Once again, Dr. Roger Frye has produced another groundbreaking book. His other works are tremendous, but I think that this new book *Financial Healing—Spiritual Foundations* is absolutely the top of the heap. While there are many practical programs from others that have helped many people in the area of finances, Roger gets to root problems that others don't even attempt to address. He provides step by step guidance of how to minister to those issues.

My appreciation for Roger and this book in particular is not just academic. I have found *Financial Healing* to be a true breakthrough book, identifying areas in my history that needed to be addressed. The result is a big step forward, moving more deeply into the abundant life that Jesus promised in John 10. It is a must read!

—The Rt. Rev. Dr. Bill Atwood,
Dean of International Affairs
Anglican Church in North America

This is book is a MUST have and a perfect accompaniment to Roger's book called *Pathway to Freedom*. My family needs this right now! This was a perfect book to go through, as a couple, with my wife. Even after years of ministering freedom and fullness to many, we received a new measure of freedom ourselves just going through this book! We have come across many folk who believe that generational iniquity doesn't exist in a Christian. Truth be told, there are a lot of things that may exist in a Christian that should not be there because the Christian allows it to operate! Ignorance is not a valid excuse for a Christian and will not stop consequences from occurring from spiritual principles in effect.

This is the perfect HOW TO manual on how to get financial victory from a spiritual perspective. Many financial courses focus on the bad fruit of financial bondage (such as habitual patterns in the flesh that need broken) but few take the ax to the root of the problem like Roger's *Financial Healing*. As you move through the book and repent/break/declare, there is no other choice but to receive healing! We can already see the change of paradigm in our thought process as it pertains to financial matters and we are rejoicing because we are aligning our thoughts with His!

Even though the focus in this book is financial, you will not be able to help but see the ripple effect moving into every part of your life. This is the Kingdom expanding within you, as you have given it permission and made room by breaking agreements handed down by generations past. Receive your healing today by going through what is written on these pages with expectancy!

—Reverend Joshua and Danielle Karlovich,
Assemblies of God, Pittsburgh, PA

My friend and ministry mentor Dr. Roger Frye just released another life changing book! The tools in this specific book have equipped us to view our financial resources quite differently. I have spent years in applying (or attempting to apply) financial principles from some of the guru's of our day including Dave Ramsey, Suze Orman, and the like. While those were both practical and helpful in their insights and practices, the teaching in this book went straight to the root of the issue. The spiritual application is such that my husband, JR, and I were uniquely impacted as it addresses the reader as an individual as well as part of the larger family system. A valuable truth teaching that will be reread for sure.

—Psychologist Kimberlee Flatt

DR. ROGER L. FRYE

HISPUBLISHING
GROUP

www.hispubg.com
A division of HISpecialists, llc

HIS Publishing Group
4310 Wiley Post Rd., Suite 201D
Addison, Texas 75001
info@hispubg.com

Library of Congress Control Number: 2016908009
ISBN-13: 978-0-9790607-4-8

Financial Healing/Dr. Roger L. Frye—2nd ed.
10 9 8 7 6 5 4 3 2

Printed in the United States of America

TABLE OF CONTENTS

ACKNOWLEDGEMENTS

I WISH TO EXPRESS MY DEEPEST GRATITUDE TO MY MENTORS OVER the years who have allowed me to soak up their wisdom and knowledge in the freedom ministry. A special thanks goes to Dr. Mickey Bonner, Dr. Henry Malone, Dr. Mark Virkler, Ed M. Smith, Chester and Betsy Kylstra, John and Paula Sandford and the Elijah House staff, Paul Cox, Arthur Burk, and other freedom ministers who have imparted their wisdom and understanding in equipping me to fulfill the role in which God has placed me.

I want to say thank you to Sheree Bates for her assistance in editing and proofreading this manuscript. I am also deeply appreciative of my other friends who offered insightful comments.

I want to say thank you to my good friend and "son" in the faith, Greg Solomon, who developed the cover design and added helpful suggestions along the way.

And finally, special thanks goes to my wife, Ruthie, who has faithfully supported my efforts in developing this material and putting it into a book form.

FOREWORD

YOU ARE GOING TO LOVE THIS BOOK! I LOVE IT BECAUSE IT IS so practical, spiritual and helpful. Experiencing God's financial blessing is something each of us hungers for. I am confident this book will guide you into experiencing more of God's financial blessings.

The book is FULL of prayers for us to pray, helping us to be released from generational sins and curses which bring financial bondage into our lives. In addition, Roger gives specific practical steps we can take to achieve financial freedom. However, the emphasis of this book is on breaking generational influences that are limiting us financially.

The prayers are specific, biblical and spiritual, and since life and death are in the power of the tongue, they are to be prayed out loud. As I prayed them I could see and feel things happening in the spiritual realm. I saw the wind of the Holy Spirit as a tornado, winding back through my generational lines, tearing up the sins and curses that were present and dispersing them so they could no longer impact my life.

I could feel the release in my spirit as I breathed out deeply. Spiritual forces were dispelled and a feeling of freedom engulfed me. I spoke this freedom over myself as I bathed in it, celebrating and welcoming it into my life. So, for me, these prayers were more than a rote mechanical reading of some black and white print.

I know a prayer must be prayed from the heart in order to be truly effective. I know how to pray a prayer from my heart. It doesn't mean grunting harder, or shouting louder, or repeating it often in a mechanical way.

Praying from my heart means I am using the language of my heart, which I understand to utilize pictures, emotion, flow and pondering/meditation. So as I prayed the prayers in this book, I prayed them using vision (seeing what I was saying), and speaking them slowly enough so I could meditate and capture the meaning of each sentence. I tuned to flow (Jn. 7:37-39), so God could bring specific things to my attention through flowing thoughts (His voice), flowing pictures (His visions) and flowing emotions (His emotions). As I did, I felt, saw and experienced many wonderful things. (We provide a scriptural basis for this definition of the language the heart, in our book, *Prayers That Heal the Heart.*)

So as you pray these prayers, pray them from your heart, and as you do, generational sins and curses will fall off as will the demonic forces connected with these sins and curses. This dismantling will offer you a new freedom to prosper financially.

I sense that this is the most spiritual book I have read on financial healing. I believe with all my heart that if you pray the prayers in this book from your heart, you will experience a new financial freedom. Try it and let me know. I love to blog out stories of people's new freedom in Christ as they step forward in faith to appropriate one more set of biblical promises.

—Dr. Mark Virkler
Founder of Communion With God Ministries
Mark@cluonline.com

Chapter One
MY JOURNEY

I WAS RAISED IN A CHRISTIAN HOME WHERE WE WENT TO CHURCH twice every Sunday and every Wednesday night for prayer meeting. We had what we called family "devotions" where the nine of us took turns reading verses out of the King James Version of the Bible and in this way we eventually covered the entire Scriptures from Genesis to Revelation. You can say that I learned to read using the Authorized Version. My parents did their best to live by Biblical principles and gave their tithe faithfully to the church ever since I can remember but, nonetheless, they struggled financially.

My dad worked in a steel factory as blue collar worker and mom did not work outside of the home. With seven of us kids there was not a lot of money to go around so mom did her best to stretch her food budget. She bought powdered milk in bulk for us to put on our cornmeal mush or oatmeal for breakfast and bought bread at the day old store, etc. But the part of living with little income that hurt was going without adequate clothing. I literally wore rags to school and sometimes my shoes were so badly worn that the soles would flap with each step I took. I remember in fourth grade standing in line after recess to go back in our room and a fellow classmate started asking about my clothes. He said, "Why do you wear clothes like this? These are the kind of clothes I throw away." I didn't have an answer for him but his words cut to the quick.

On another occasion in the summer, between third and fourth grade, I went to Indiana to spend several months with my biological father and his wife. We were riding in the car, I was in the back seat, and stepmom asked, "Why do you have such raggedy worn out clothes?" Her words hurt but to save face I lied and said, "Oh, I have plenty of good clothes at home in California." She and my dad made eye contact and communicated that my mom packed such clothes so that they would have to buy me new ones.

As I look back on the situation growing up, I suspect that mom had developed a poverty mentality and that the spirit of poverty took over many of the day-to-day decisions she made. She could have looked for deals on clothes for us kids. One can often find clothes in a thrift store that are almost new and cost next to nothing. I believe it began for her as a girl growing up in Wisconsin. Her mother, out of fear, sold their farm for pennies on the dollar. Grandma feared that if she stayed another winter in that cold climate that she would not survive. They put the farm up for sale and month after month no offers came in. They kept reducing the asking price until finally, out of desperation and fear, she sold the home and land for a mere pittance and headed to the West Coast to start a new life in a warmer climate.

To earn a living the whole family worked as migrant workers picking vegetables, fruit, and nuts. Those migrant camps often proved to be rough situations, especially for a teenage girl. On top of those harsh living and working conditions my mom had to cope with a stepfather who viciously abused her physically. To escape that environment, at age 17, mom married the first man that came along who showed some interest. Sadly, her first husband revealed his true colors as he too mistreated her. He abused her by his unfaithfulness. She suspected he'd had an affair with a mutual friend, Letha. He wanted to keep BOTH my mom and Letha, and obviously my mom said no way. After divorcing him she had to support her two children by herself without any child support payments. With this backdrop it is easy to understand why mom developed the expectation that she would always struggle financially, and that she would have to learn how to survive on next to nothing.

As much as I hated poor conditions, I too developed the same expectation and in addition made an inner vow that I would never struggle financially. I married Ruthie at age 22 and, even though we paid our bills, we always struggled to make ends meet. From early on in our marriage we committed to tithing and gave up and above the tithe to worthy causes. Yet, finances remained tight. I'll never forget the time Ruthie and I were totally out of groceries and had no money to buy more. We prayed earnestly for God's provision. After praying Ruthie looked up at the top of the kitchen cabinet and asked, "What is that?" We had never seen it before even though we had lived in that apartment for several months. I climbed up there to take a closer look and, to our amazement, someone had placed a wad of cash up there. Needless to say, we had our grocery money. I could tell you other stories of miraculous provision over the years but still, as a general rule, we suffered from financial lack. Even though we might get a little bit ahead, something would always happen that would devour our finances.

You might respond by saying we needed better financial planning. Yes, I agree that good financial planning is a discipline needed in every person's life but we did plan. We carefully followed a budget and refused frivolous spending, living a very modest life-style but sometimes our best laid plans fail. For years I diligently put money away in my retirement account knowing that through compound interest it would grow into a nice nest egg to help support us in the sunset years. However, after losing my job the financial stress became so great that we felt it was necessary to cash in early even though it meant early withdrawal penalties. Later we developed a plan to buy one house a year. We would live in it a year, fix it up, and rent it out, buy another house and live in it for a year and then rent it out and so on until we had a good number of rental houses. As a pastor I had an income tax advantage in that the church gave us a tax free housing allowance. The only taxes due were for social security and Medicare. Once the mortgages were paid off we would live off the rent money or gradually sell the homes after we retired. The plan was working well with the first two houses, then the economy tanked, my job situation changed, and real estate laws tightened up making it harder to continue with our plan.

The legendary boxer Joe Louis said, "Everyone has a plan until they get hit." Later Mike Tyson offered his own rendition saying, "Everyone has a plan until they get punched in the face." As you can see, my life story will attest to that. Planning is always good but there are other spiritual factors involved that must be dealt with. No matter what plan you develop, there is no guarantee that you will become rich or successful in the eyes of the world.

Many motivational speakers like to say that where we're at in our life is because of the decisions we have made. And that the level of success we have reached is no more than a collection of all the decisions and actions we've made up to this time in our life. And that we never become successful without first taking responsibility for our current conditions. There is an element of truth in what they say but does their teaching represent the whole truth? What about the spiritual dynamic? What about the not wrestling with flesh and blood teaching in Ephesians chapter six? What about faith? And where does God fit in this financial success teaching?

About eight years ago Ruthie and I prayed to systematically break financial curses. It was subtle at first but gradually we became aware of the fact that the financial ravaging had ceased and things got much easier. Success with finances for the Christian requires a strong work ethic, careful planning, obedient giving, and disciplined spending. But many believers do all these right things and yet, suffer from persistent financial shortage. In these cases financial curses must be dealt with and I believe God wants all His children free from financial ravaging and destruction.

When I speak about breaking financial curses don't get the idea that this is some get rich scheme or that I'm suggesting you'll never have financial challenges. Breaking financial curses is no substitute for good old common sense and doing your due diligence before spending or investing. Keep in mind that God wants His children to have enough money to meet all their needs and have plenty left over to sow into the lives of other people. His will is not for every believer to be filthy rich but that we have enough and that we live in contentment. For some that necessitates the breaking of financial curses.

Over my many years of ministry I have seen people who persistently struggled financially. For many of them it is a life-style issue. They buy merchandise and services they simply cannot afford. They consistently overspend or practice impulse buying. There is a spiritual reason people possess these negative character issues and by going through this material you may experience a big personality makeover.

Besides breaking these financial curses another reason Christians don't get a financial breakthrough is because they have not been sowing into the Kingdom of God. Those who will get the greatest benefit from this teaching are those who have been faithful to give by faith and out of love for the Lord. If you have been giving in this way for a long time and have not received a financial breakthrough that means there is a dam blocking the blessings ready to be released. These financial curses can curse your blessings so that you can't receive to the extent that God has planned for you. The Bible talks about our blessings being cursed. Malachi 2:2 states, *"If you will not listen, if you will not take it to heart to give honor to my name, says the LORD of hosts, then I will send the curse upon you and I will curse your blessings. Indeed, I have already cursed them, because you do not lay it to heart."* So if you have not yet committed to being a generous giver I encourage you to do so today.

WHAT DOES GIVING GENEROUSLY PRODUCE FOR THE GIVER?

According to 2 Corinthians chapter nine the Bible says this about generosity: you will reap generously, receive God's love, God will provide all you need, you will always have plenty to share, becoming permanently generous, your good deeds will be remembered forever, your giving proves you are obedient to the Good News of Christ, and those who receive your gift will pray for you with deep affection.

I love the way the Message Bible puts it,

Remember: A stingy planter gets a stingy crop; a lavish planter gets a lavish crop. I want each of you to take plenty of time to think it over, and make up your own mind what you will give. That will protect you against sob stories and arm-twisting. God loves it when the giver delights in the giving.

God can pour on the blessings in astonishing ways so that you're ready for anything and everything, more than just ready to do what needs to be done. As one psalmist puts it,

> *He throws caution to the winds,*
> *giving to the needy in reckless abandon.*
> *His right-living, right-giving ways*
> *never run out, never wear out.*

This most generous God who gives seed to the farmer that becomes bread for your meals is more than extravagant with you. He gives you something you can then give away, which grows into full-formed lives, robust in God, wealthy in every way, so that you can be generous in every way, producing with us great praise to God. (2 Corinthians 9:6-11, MSG).

I pastored a church years ago where a group of us went out to eat after the last Sunday morning service. A dear woman of God, whose name I will not mention, went with us nearly every Sunday. And almost every Sunday she would say, "I only give God ten percent so I'm sure not going to give the waiter more than ten percent." Ouch! I bet those waiters loved to see her coming. In retrospect, she may have repeated this saying so often because her conscience was bothering her. I believe that Christians should not have a stingy attitude but should be known for their generosity. The world will know we are Christians by our love and generous giving is an expression of love.

I'm excited for you as you begin this journey of living out your God-ordained destiny regarding financial matters.

Chapter Two

WISDOM FOR FINANCIAL VICTORY

HARRY TRUMAN SAID, "IT'S A RECESSION WHEN YOUR NEIGHBOR loses his job; it's a depression when you lose your own." What do I do in light of the economic turndown and potential of losing my job? How can I best manage my personal finances when there is too much month at the end of the money? How do I live victoriously for Christ with all the cultural pressures to live independent of Him? I believe there is one word that makes all the difference—one word that will make us or break us—one word that will produce a fulfilling and exciting new venture with God. And we all need to experience this one word if we want to enjoy all that God has for us. It is what the Apostle Paul prayed for constantly for the Christians at Ephesus. What is that one word? It is "wisdom."

What is wisdom? It is more than just common sense. Some sage remarked, "Common sense is what keeps a horse from betting on a track meet." That's horse sense. But wisdom is more than common sense, it is uncommon sense. Dictionary.com defines wisdom as "knowledge of what is true or right coupled with just judgment as to action; sagacity, discernment, or insight." I think this definition pretty much nails it but the Bible has much more to say about this subject.

Wisdom is not synonymous with head knowledge. Rather true wisdom is a product of the Spirit. Some things in life cannot be learned—they must be given. Wisdom is a spiritual virtue given by God. In Ephesians 1:17 it is referred to as the "spirit of wisdom," *that the God of our Lord Jesus Christ, the Father of glory, may give to you the spirit of wisdom and revelation in the knowledge of Him.* In Luke 2:40 Jesus is described as, "filled with the Spirit and with wisdom." In Isaiah 11 the Holy Spirit is referred to as the Spirit of wisdom along with six other characteristics. Joshua was full of "the spirit of wisdom" (Deut. 34:9). Wisdom is a very spiritual thing. Luke says that Jesus grew in wisdom. In the days of His flesh He needed wisdom and if the sinless Son of God grew in wisdom how much more do we need it?

At age 68 I'm a whole lot wiser than I was at 28 and thank God I've grown in wisdom. Here are the top seven lessons I've learned over the years.

THE TOP SEVEN LESSONS I'VE LEARNED OVER THE YEAR.

1) Never ask a woman when the baby's due unless you know for certain that she is in fact pregnant.

2) Even though you mean it in a nice way, never, ever say to a pregnant woman, even though she's a good friend, "Man, you're getting big!"

3) In the morning never ask your wife if she's fixed her hair yet.

4) Never buy your wife a book on dieting for her birthday.

5) Always wear your glasses when you brush your teeth. Never assume that just because there's a tube of something on the bathroom counter that it is toothpaste. It just might be Ben-Gay. Yuk!

6) Never rub your eyes or go to the bathroom right after chopping jalapeño peppers.

7) NEVER UNDER ANY CIRCUMSTANCES take a sleeping pill and a laxative on the same night.

Looking back, those kind of lessons are funny but, on a more serious note, I think we all want wisdom, but what is it? Someone said, "Wisdom is knowing as much at 46 as you thought you knew at 18." I read a book some years ago on Wicca (witchcraft) by a man who is a former Wiccan. He said something that interested me. I used to think that the reason most people got into witchcraft was primarily for power. That is part of it, but according to this author, the main reason people get into it is for wisdom. In their PR Wiccans say that the word "Wicca" means wise, or "wise one." People want wisdom and will even get into witchcraft to get it.

What is wisdom? Is it the same as knowledge? Is wisdom really just another name for knowledge?

Knowledge is closely aligned with wisdom. Scripture makes it clear that they often go together—but you can be knowledgeable and yet unwise. We want wisdom and knowledge. But knowledge in the biblical sense is a knowing of God and His ways experientially. It is not book learning, it is an intimate knowledge. I have a knowledge of Ruthie but I didn't get it by studying books about her, I got it by spending time with her.

A person may have every earned degree and course of study in every educational institution and still not possess wisdom. Here is another definition of wisdom: "the capacity to assimilate and appropriate learning prudently." But wisdom is more than that. Godly wisdom is the ability to receive and apply spiritual truth. There is no real wisdom apart from God, because wisdom is seeing life from God's point of view. It is being able to detect God's hand in our everyday circumstances and face them in a godly way. Wisdom is what is true and right combined with good judgment. That's wisdom! And that's the wisdom that James encourages us to seek. In James 3:17 we are told this, *But the wisdom that comes from heaven is first of all pure; then peace-loving, considerate, submissive, full of mercy and good fruit, impartial and sincere.*

Can you imagine God appearing before you and asking, "Is there anything in the world you would like for Me to do for you? What do you want? It is yours for the asking"? What would you ask Him for? A hungry person would probably ask for food, an impoverished man would likely request money and a sick person might ask for health.

God did ask someone that question—King Solomon. *On that night God appeared to Solomon, and said to him, "Ask! What shall I give you?"* (2 Chron. 1:7). What an opportunity! God said, "Solomon, take your pick. Whatever you want is yours for the asking."

What did Solomon request? Fame? Fortune? Power? Pleasure? Women? No, even though all of these became his (and often to his embarrassment and shame) he asked for wisdom.

Read carefully his request recorded in 2 Chron. 1:10. *Now give me wisdom and knowledge, that I may go out and come in before this people; for who can judge this great people of Yours? God answered, Because this was in your heart, and you have not asked riches or wealth or honor or the life of your enemies, nor have you asked long life—but have asked wisdom and knowledge for yourself, that you may judge my people, over whom I have made you king— wisdom and knowledge is granted you; and I will give you riches and wealth and honor, such as none of the kings have had that have been before you, neither shall there any after you have the like.* I think God liked what Solomon asked for, don't you?

Solomon asked for the right gift in the right manner and the book of Proverbs contains a collection of the wisdom God granted King Solomon three millennia ago. It is imperative that we walk in wisdom especially when it comes to financial matters.

I ran a word search using my Bible software. It pulled up 215 verses that include the word "wisdom" and 180 verses that contain the word "wise." That's 395 times! So do you think wisdom is important to God? Proverbs 16:16 states, *How much better to get wisdom than gold! And to get understanding is to be chosen rather than silver.*

If wisdom is so important how do we get it? Here are some necessary steps to help in this matter.

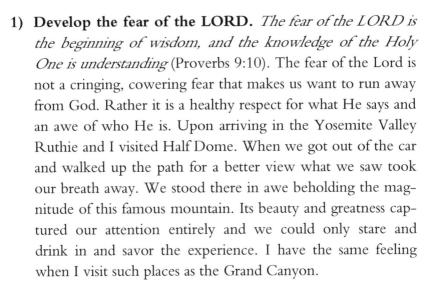

1) **Develop the fear of the LORD.** *The fear of the LORD is the beginning of wisdom, and the knowledge of the Holy One is understanding* (Proverbs 9:10). The fear of the Lord is not a cringing, cowering fear that makes us want to run away from God. Rather it is a healthy respect for what He says and an awe of who He is. Upon arriving in the Yosemite Valley Ruthie and I visited Half Dome. When we got out of the car and walked up the path for a better view what we saw took our breath away. We stood there in awe beholding the magnitude of this famous mountain. Its beauty and greatness captured our attention entirely and we could only stare and drink in and savor the experience. I have the same feeling when I visit such places as the Grand Canyon.

These kinds of experiences represent a little taste of what it is to behold the beauty and majesty of the Lord. When we get a glimpse of who God is, the only thing we can do is stand in awe of Him. That is the fear of the Lord. *Let all the earth fear the LORD; let all the inhabitants of the world stand in awe of Him* (Psalm 33:8).

The writer of Proverbs adds another dynamic to understanding the fear of the Lord. He says, The fear of the Lord is to hate evil (Proverbs 8:13a). To fear the Lord means that we hate the things that God hates because we see their destructive nature. Another way to put it is we see the evil in the evil and we do all to avoid it. To hate evil is to turn away from it because we understand how it hurts the heart of God and wounds people. *Behold, the fear of the Lord, that is wisdom, and to depart from evil is understanding* (Job 28:28). *And by the fear of the LORD men depart from evil* (Proverbs 16:6b).

God promises many blessings if we will only fear Him. Not only do we receive wisdom, we receive protection and blessings on our finances. Here are some powerful promises on the finances of those who fear Him: *Praise the LORD! Blessed is the man who fears the LORD, who delights greatly in His commandments. His descendants will be mighty on earth; the generation of the upright will be blessed. Wealth and riches will be in his house, and his righteousness endures forever* (Psalm 112:1-3). *By humility and the fear of the LORD are riches, and honor, and life* (Proverbs 22:4). God blesses our finances when we truly fear Him.

2) **Ask God for wisdom.** That's what it says in James 1:5-6. *If any of you lacks wisdom, let him ask of God, who gives to all liberally and without reproach, and it will be given to him. 6 But let him ask in faith, with no doubting, for he who doubts is like a wave of the sea driven and tossed by the wind.* We have not because we ask not and one reason for unanswered prayer is unoffered prayer but we must ask in faith. Scripture calls Jesus the wisdom of God so that means that Jesus is our wisdom and Jesus lives in all believers. Therefore we can ask Jesus to release His wisdom through us.

3) **Meditate on God's Word.** Meditation seems to be a lost art in the church today. The psalmist cried out, *Oh, how I love Your law! It is my meditation all the day. You, through Your commandments, make me wiser than my enemies* (Psalm 119:97, emphasis added). When Joshua was getting ready to lead the Children of Israel into the Promised Land I'm sure he experienced some intense anxiety. That's why God appeared to him and said, *This Book of the Law shall not depart from your mouth, but you shall meditate in it day and night, that you may observe to do according to all that is written in it. For then you will make your way prosperous, and then you will have good success* (Joshua 1:8). God promised Joshua that He would prosper him if he practiced Biblical meditation and obeyed Him.

The way I meditate on Scripture is that I go over and over a passage emphasizing a different word each time through. I ask God to speak to me the truths He wants me to receive at the heart level. I speak the Bible passage out loud until it gets down in my heart. Biblical meditation has been the most significant discipline to transform my life.

4) Sit under the teaching of wise people. The Bible speaks of the need for wise counsel. *For by wise counsel you will wage your own war, and in a multitude of counselors there is safety.* (Proverbs 24:6). Before making a large purchase run it by your spiritual authorities. I realize that "A large purchase" is a relative term but for me it would be around five thousand or more but for you it might be more or less. If you've had a history of getting in debt over your head I suggest you have a spiritual advisor to whom you submit all of your purchases.

5) Do what God says. The two conditions for receiving the blessings of God are,

a) Listen to the Lord
and
b) Do what He says.

Do you want wisdom to have a better marriage? Do what God has clearly said. "Husbands love your wives as Christ loved the church. Wives respect your husbands." As we do what God has clearly told us to do He blesses us by giving us more wisdom and understanding. God is not interested in subsidizing our disobedience. As the psalmist said, *I understand more than the ancients, because I keep Your precepts* (Psalm 119:100).

Do you want wisdom to better manage your finances? Do what God has outlined in Scripture—give Him the first fruits of all your increase. I have found that when I give God the first ten percent of my income that He gives me wisdom to make the 90 percent go further than the 100 percent. This doesn't make sense in the natural but remember the spiritual is more real than the natural and wisdom is spiritual. 1 Corinthians speaks of godly wisdom versus human wisdom. If we use human wisdom, the ways of God don't make sense just like the cross doesn't make sense to the human mind.

JOURNALING

In addition to obeying the clear commands of God in His Word regarding our finances there are other ways to get direction from God. I suggest that you learn to journal and dialogue with God about your finances. Years ago while browsing in a Christian book store, by "chance" I happened to come across a book that changed my life. It was written by Mark and Patti Virkler and entitled "Dialogue with God." Many years ago God had radically changed Mark's life by showing him some Biblical principles that enabled him to discern God's still small voice.

Mark points his readers to a passage of Scripture found in Habakkuk chapter two, verses one and two where we read, *I will stand my watch and set myself on the rampart, and watch to see what He will say to me, and what I will answer when I am corrected. Then the LORD answered me and said: "Write the vision and make it plain on tablets, that he may run who reads it."* From these verses Mark discovered four keys to hearing God's voice. Let me put this teaching in my own words.

First, Habakkuk quieted himself. He got away from distractions, away from the hubbub of the marketplace and friends. The psalmist said, *Be still, and know that I am God; I will be exalted among the nations, I will be exalted in the earth! (Psalm 46:10).* The expanded version of this verse is: *Be still, cease striving, let go, and relax and know that I am God.* God often speaks in a still small voice so when we have a lot of noise and interruptions going on around us it becomes difficult to discern what God is saying. Find a quiet place and still yourself and relax. Taking a few deep breaths from the diaphragm usually proves helpful. The first key to hearing God's voice is to still yourself.

Then Habakkuk made a very curious statement. He said he would, "watch to see what He will say to me." You would think that he would say, "listen to hear what He will say," but instead he said "watch." From this word "watch" we get the second key and that is to tune to vision. The writer of Hebrews said, "Looking unto Jesus, the author and finisher of our faith" (Hebrews 12:2). We need to keep our eyes on Jesus because pure words flow from the vision we hold before our eyes. A good way to do this is to recall a favorite Gospel story. When we read or hear a Gospel story we see it being played out in our mind's eye.

The story of the prophet Balaam illustrates the problem of focusing on an idol and how it leads to impure prophetic words. Balaam was known in the then-known world as a powerful prophet and Balak, the king of the Moabites, wanted to hire him to come and curse the Children of Israel. So Balak sent a contingent of men to Balaam offering riches and honor. Before Balaam agreed to do so he did the right thing and prayed asking God whether or not he should go. God clearly answered and told him absolutely not, do not go with them.

They journeyed back to Balak with the news that Balaam had refused to come. Balak was not deterred so he sent another contingent of men more prestigious than the first offering more riches and honor than the first group. What did Balaam do? He went and prayed, asking God whether or not he should go with them. But why did he have to pray again if God had clearly told him not to go? It's because his eyes were fixed on the riches and honor. The second time he prayed he thought he heard God say, "Yes, go ahead and go with them but only say what I tell you to say." On the surface that "word" sounds religious and good but why did God suddenly change His mind?

It wasn't God's perfect will for him to go with these men but when we harden our hearts and stubbornly go in the direction we want to go, God usually lets us do it and then suffer the consequences. In Jude, verse 11 we read, *Woe to them! For they have gone in the way of Cain, have run greedily in the error of Balaam for profit, and perished in the rebellion of Korah.* Here Jude is describing apostates, false prophets, and false teachers who crept into the church. One characteristic of such individuals is that they do what they do for profit and Jude uses Balaam as an example from the Old Testament. It's clear that when Balaam prayed the second time around he had his eyes on the reward, the money, the profit, instead of on God and that reward became an idol to him. And consequently, he received an impure word from the LORD. So the second key to hearing God's voice is fix your eyes on Jesus and don't look to an idol whatever that idol may be.

The third key comes from the Hebrew word for prophecy, *naba*, which means literally "to bubble up." In the Old Testament when prophets received a prophetic word from God often the words would bubble up from their human spirit as the Holy Spirit spoke. Words bubble up from our spirit into our mind so that we can express them. Discerning these words is a right brain activity and if that is the case we need to activate the right hemisphere of our brain. Right brain activities involve the intuitive, artsy, creative part of our being. Walking through the woods, listening to soft worship music, singing spontaneous words to God, sitting in your garden are examples of activities that activate the right side of the brain. People who are stuck in the left side of their brain, the logical, analytical, reasoning hemisphere, usually have a hard time hearing God's voice. Often, when God speaks to us, spontaneous thoughts will alight upon our mind but we need to tune in to those thoughts. The third key is to tune to the spontaneous flow of thoughts that come into your mind. Tune to flow.

The fourth key comes from what God told Habakkuk and that was to write it down. There's a real beauty in writing down the spontaneous flow of thoughts. For many of us, when we get spontaneous thoughts like that we judge those thoughts before the flow ends. We think, "Is that me or is that God?" "Is that God or is that the devil trying to confuse me?" "Is that the result of too much pizza?" And when we start judging the thoughts before the flow stops we cut off the flow prematurely. But if we keep in mind that we're writing it down and we can judge the thoughts later it frees us to stay tuned to the flow of spontaneous thoughts. By writing it down we have a record of what God said. Then I can judge the words I received as to whether or not they contradict the teachings of Scripture, whether or not they go against the revealed nature and attributes of God. By writing it down I can take those words and submit them to several trusted spiritual advisors to corroborate that they are truly from God.

Mark Virkler calls this journaling. In your journal write down a question to ask God. For example, you might write in your journal, "Lord, what do You want to say to me about how I'm handling my finances?" Or, "Lord, what do You want to say to me about how I can save money?" Or, "Heavenly Father, what do You want to say to me about this boat I want to buy?" Then still yourself, fix your eyes on Jesus, tune to flow, and write down what you hear. Through this method of dialoguing with God and submitting your journal to a trusted advisor you will gain wisdom in handling your finances.

In your journal make a list of your financial problems. Then make a new list ranking them from most important to least important. Now quiet yourself before God and with pen in hand journal and ask God what He wants to say, beginning with the most difficult problems. In this way we are giving God our problems and seeking Him for guidance and wisdom. As you make this list be as honest and open as you possibly can. You may need to repent for your bad decisions and poor choices.

Many of our poor choices in financial matters involve a presuming on the future. James says this about presuming on the future: *Come now, you who say, "Today or tomorrow we will go to such and such a city, spend a year there, buy and sell, and make a profit"; 14 whereas you do not know what will happen tomorrow. For what is your life? It is even a vapor that appears for a little time and then vanishes away. 15 Instead you ought to say, "If the Lord wills, we shall live and do this or that" (James 4:13-15).* When I willfully and recklessly overspend and go in debt I am presuming on the future, the very thing that James warns against.

It's easy to see our self as a victim and the victim mentality will hold us in financial bondage. We need to break the victim mentality and we begin to do that through confession and repentance. God didn't make us to be victims but to be victors. Say these words out loud, "I am a new creation in Christ Jesus. I am forgiven and cleansed by His blood. The old me has passed away and all things have become new. Jesus lives in me and greater is He who is in me than he who is in the world. My heavenly Father loves me with a perfect, unfailing love. I am loved. I am kept by His blood. I am accepted. I am not a victim. I am an overcomer through Him who loves me. The very same Spirit that raised Jesus from the dead, lives in me, in Jesus' Name." It is imperative that we break the victim mentality because the victim spirit will hold us in poverty.

Once you break the victim mentality, let the Holy Spirit search your heart and become brutally honest about the sins which led to your current financial mess. We need to see our sins before we can confess them and God promises to forgive all sin that we confess. True repentance involves a humbling of ourselves before God. When we humbly face our own shortcomings it does something to dismantle pride. Pride is a big one because the Bible says that God resists the proud but give grace to the humble. I don't know about you but I want God's grace when it comes to my financial issues.

There are other ways God speaks to us about our finances. For example, one time I had a rental house that I rented to a single mom with three kids. After living there about a year she gave notice that she was moving out. When she got all of her belongings out of the house I went there to do an inspection to determine what had to be done to get it ready to rent it out to another renter. To my dismay I found a number of things that needed fixing. For instance, her dog dug deep holes all over in the back yard and nearly chewed completely through the air conditioner cable. My plan was to keep her security deposit to offset the cost of repairs. That night I had a very vivid dream in which God told me to give almost all of the deposit back to her. I obeyed the Lord and I'm sure that money was a big help to that struggling single mom. The Bible is full of dreams. For instance, as we read the story about the birth of Jesus in the Gospel of Matthew we discover five dreams surrounding that event. And God still speaks to His people through dreams so we need to pay attention to our dreams.

God desires to give us wisdom but we need to listen to His voice and obey. Luke tells the story about when Jesus was teaching the multitudes from a boat a little bit from the shore. When He was finished teaching he told Peter to launch out into the deep water and let down his nets for a catch. Keep in mind that Peter was a seasoned fisherman and knew his business well. So he protested at first saying, *Master, we have toiled all night and caught nothing; nevertheless at Your word I will let down the net.* Based on Peter's human wisdom Jesus' words didn't make sense. They fished at the best time of the day to catch fish and came up empty-handed. But out of deference to Jesus he let down the net and to his astonishment he caught so many fish that the net was breaking. He signaled to his partners in another boat to come and help. Both boats were filled to the point that they were beginning to sink. To those fishermen that was an amazing miracle and God wants to perform financial miracles for His people but the condition is that we listen and obey.

PRAYER FOR WISDOM

"Lord, You said You would give us wisdom if we ask in faith so, God, I'm asking. I repent for those in my generational line and for me for not honoring Your wisdom. I receive Your wisdom now, in Jesus' Name, Amen."

Chapter Three
FREEDOM FROM FINANCIAL
INIQUITY AND SIN

PEOPLE IN OUR GENERATIONAL LINE MAY HAVE COMMITTED
sins related to finances that brought iniquity into our lives which
hinders our ability to make money, save money and use money wisely. According to Scripture, iniquity gets passed on to the third and
fourth generation. *"For I the LORD your God, am a jealous God,
visiting the iniquity of the fathers on the children to the third and
fourth generations of those who hate Me"* (Exodus 20:5, NKJV).
Children suffer from the sins of their fathers. After David sinned with
Bathsheba, 2 Samuel 12:19 says,

> *When David saw that his servants were whispering,
> David perceived that the child was dead. Therefore
> David said to his servants, "Is the child dead?" And
> they said, "He is dead."*

Financial iniquity brought into our bloodline by the sins of our
ancestors allows Satan to claim legal right to put a curse on our finances. The good news, however, is that it is fairly easy to break
these curses, thus, bringing freedom to receive and keep the finances
God intends us to have, to save money, and to use it wisely.

There are references in Scripture about confessing the sins of our
ancestors. Daniel confessed the sins of his fathers as well as the sins of
the nation (Dan. 9:3-17). Nehemiah also confessed the sins of his
fathers.

Both my father's house and I have sinned. We have acted very corruptly against You, and have not kept the commandments, the statutes, the ordinances which You have commanded Your servant Moses (Neh. 1:6c–7).

The Israelites also confessed the sins of their fathers.

Then those of Israelite lineage separated themselves from all foreigners; and they stood and confessed their sins and the iniquities of their fathers (Nehemiah 9:2).

Let me relate this to our financial issues. Habitual, unrepented financial sins that your ancestors stubbornly committed can allow Satan to place a financial curse on you. But be of good courage. You don't have to stay in bondage to the iniquity of your forefathers. Through confession and renunciation we can break the hold of any financial curse or iniquity that we've inherited.

According to the *Theological Wordbook of the Old Testament*[1] the Hebrew word for iniquity is *āwa* or *āwōn* which means "bend," "twist," "distort," "perversion," "iniquity," or "punishment for guilt." The word conveys the thought of both the deed and its consequences, the offense and its penalty. It is a sin pattern that demands punishment. When Cain killed his brother, Abel, he showed no remorse for his sin. When God asked him where his brother was Cain replied, "Am I my brother's keeper?" Based on this story, another way to understand iniquity is that it is a twisted response to God for our specific sin. So God curses Cain for his transgression and Cain responds by saying, "My punishment is too great!" The word for "punishment" in this passage is the word, *āwōn* and can be translated as, "My iniquity, or my twistedness, is too great." The word can refer to his twistedness or the punishment that comes with his twistedness. This twisting of Cain's sin and the penalty involved is what got passed on to his descendants.

Someone will object to this teaching saying that the concept of suffering for the iniquities of our forefathers was an Old Testament idea and no longer holds true for the Christian today. But notice the words of Jesus in Luke 11:47-50,

> *Woe to you! For you build the tombs of the prophets whom your fathers killed. 48 So you are witnesses and you consent to the deeds of your fathers, for they killed them, and you build their tombs. 49 Therefore also the Wisdom of God said, 'I will send them prophets and apostles, some of whom they will kill and persecute,' 50 so that the blood of all the prophets, shed from the foundation of the world, may be charged against this generation (ESV).*

Here Jesus is addressing the Pharisees and the Lawyers and telling them that since they inherited the sins of their forefathers, they will be held responsible for them since they endorsed them by doing the same thing. Iniquity causes a propensity, a drawing, to do the same things our ancestors did. The truth is that iniquity does get passed down through the generations and this dynamic is often called "generational iniquity." One way to identify generational iniquity regarding our finances is to look for negative patterns that occur repeatedly throughout our family line. The probability that one or more of your ancestors habitually committed all of the following sins is quite high. Therefore, I suggest that you assume they are there in your bloodline. If you confess a generational sin and it's not there it won't hurt you, but if it is there and you confess it you will gain more freedom. It is necessary to identify with the sins of your ancestors and, as a representative of your family line, confess and repent of these sins.

CONFESSION OF SINS RELATED TO FINANCES

SAY THIS OUT LOUD:
"In Jesus' Name, I confess and renounce the sin of
_____ in the lives of my generations past." Name all of
the following sins.

Ungodly usury. Exodus 22:25. *If you lend money to any of My people who are poor among you, you shall not be like a moneylender to him; you shall not charge him interest.*

Bribes taken against the innocent. Psalm 15:5. *He who does not put out his money at usury, nor does he take a bribe against the innocent. He who does these things shall never be moved.* Deut. 27:25. *Cursed is the one who takes a bribe to slay an innocent person. And all the people shall say, "Amen!"*

Worshipping of money and the "love of money." 1 Timothy 6:10. *For the love of money is a root of all kinds of evil, for which some have strayed from the faith in their greediness, and pierced themselves through with many sorrows.* This verse represents one of the most often misquoted passages in the Bible. It doesn't say, "Money is the root of all evil." It says, "The love of money is the root of all kinds of evil."

Not paying earned wages. James 5:4. *Indeed the wages of the laborers who mowed your fields, which you kept back by fraud, cry out; and the cries of the reapers have reached the ears of the Lord of Sabaoth.*

Shedding of innocent blood. Gen. 4:12. *When you till the ground, it shall no longer yield its strength to you. A fugitive and a vagabond you shall be on the earth.* The context is that Cain murdered his brother Abel. Say, "In Jesus' Name, I break the curse of wandering."

Disobedience to God. Deuteronomy 28:45. *Moreover all these curses shall come upon you and pursue and overtake you, until you are destroyed, because you did not obey the voice of the Lord your*

God, to keep His commandments and His statutes which He commanded you.

Not serving the LORD joyfully and gladly in times of prosperity. Deuteronomy 28:47-48. *Because you did not serve the LORD your God with joy and gladness of heart, for the abundance of everything,* [48] *therefore you shall serve your enemies, whom the LORD will send against you, in hunger, in thirst, in nakedness, and in need of everything; and He will put a yoke of iron on your neck until He has destroyed you.*

Idolatry. 1 John 5:21. Little children, keep yourselves from idols. Hosea 8:7. *They sow the wind, and reap the whirlwind. The stalk has no bud; it shall never produce meal. If it should produce, aliens would swallow it up.* Note: the context of Hosea 8:7 is the making of idols. An idol is anything you look to for security or self-worth other than Jesus.

Stubbornness. 1 Samuel 15:23a. *For rebellion is as the sin of witchcraft, and stubbornness is as iniquity and idolatry.* Stubbornness is as idolatry and carries the same consequences. One example is that a person may become set in his own ways, relying on his own will rather than on God's instructions regarding finances.

Sexual sins. Proverbs 5:10 (CEV). *Strangers will get your money and everything else you have worked for.* Note: the context here is that of a man going after an immoral woman.

Refusing or neglecting to tithe. Malachi 3:8-10. *"Will a man rob God? Yet you have robbed Me! But you say, 'In what way have we robbed You?' In tithes and offerings.* [9] *You are cursed with a curse, for you have robbed Me, even this whole nation.* [10] *Bring all the tithes into the storehouse, that there may be food in My house, and try Me now in this,"* Says the LORD *of hosts, "If I will not open for you the windows of heaven and pour out for you such blessing that there will not be room enough to receive it."*

Covetousness. Exodus 20:17. *You shall not covet your neighbor's house; you shall not covet your neighbor's wife, nor his male servant, nor his female servant, nor his ox, nor his donkey, nor anything that is your neighbor's.*

Not trusting God for provision. Psalm 54:4. God is my helper! The Lord is the provider for my life. God's Word© Translation. One of the Names of God is Jehovah-Jireh, which means "God is my provider, my source, my sufficiency."

Fearing that you will lose everything or **Fear of Poverty.** Job 3:25. For the thing I greatly feared has come upon me, and what I dreaded has happened to me.

Fearing that you will not be provided for. Isaiah 41:10. *Fear not, for I am with you; be not dismayed, for I am your God. I will strengthen you, yes, I will help you, I will uphold you with My righteous right hand.*

Fear of failure. Proverbs 26:13. *The lazy man says, "There is a lion in the road! A fierce lion is in the streets!"* Fear leads to laziness and laziness leads to lack.

Slothfulness. Proverbs 12:24. *The hand of the diligent will rule, but the lazy man will be put to forced labor.*

Trusting in earthly riches above trusting in God. Proverbs 11:28. *He who trusts in his riches will fall, but the righteous will flourish like foliage.*

Selling one's soul in exchange for riches. Matthew 16:26. For what profit is it to a man if he gains the whole world, and loses his own soul? Or what will a man give in exchange for his soul?

Seeking riches over a good name. Proverbs 22:1. *A good name is to be chosen rather than great riches, loving favor rather than silver and gold.*

Allowing earthly possessions to choke out the desire for God. Luke 8:14. *Now the ones that fell among thorns are those who,* *when they have heard, go out and are choked with cares, riches, and pleasures of life, and bring no fruit to maturity.*

Acquiring riches through unrighteous means such as lying, stealing or cheating. Proverbs 10:2 (CEV). *What you gain by doing evil won't help you at all, but being good can save you from death."* Proverbs 11:1. *"Dishonest scales are an abomination to the LORD, but a just weight is His delight.*

Not fearing God. Psalm 34:9. *Oh, fear the LORD, you His saints! There is no want to those who fear Him.*

Not seeking God or passivity towards God. Psalm 34:10. *The young lions lack and suffer hunger; but those who seek the LORD shall not lack any good thing.* Do you seek God with all your heart?

Recklessly acquiring debt. Proverbs 22:7. *The rich rules over the poor, and the borrower is servant to the lender.*

Not repaying debts. Psalm 37:21. *The wicked borrows and does not repay, but the righteous shows mercy and gives.*

Stinginess and lack of mercy. Psalm 37:21b. *but the righteous shows mercy and gives.*

Living above your means. Luke 14:28-29. *For which of you, intending to build a tower, does not sit down first and count the cost, whether he has enough to finish it— lest, after he has laid the foundation, and is not able to finish, all who see it begin to mock him,*

Coming into agreement with the spirit of poverty. Philippians 4:19. *And my God will supply every need of yours according to his riches in glory in Christ Jesus.* Remember, God wants us to have all of our needs met with plenty left over to sow into the lives of other people.

Self-Sufficiency. Proverbs 3:5-6. *Trust in the LORD with all your heart, and lean not on your own understanding; In all your ways acknowledge Him, and He shall direct your paths.*

Not seeking godly counsel. Proverbs 15:22. *Plans fail for lack of counsel, but with many advisers they succeed* (NIV). Sometimes we just don't see the solution to our financial crisis and we need to seek a godly person who has wisdom for counsel.

Boastfulness over income and wealth. Proverbs 16:18-19. *Pride goes before destruction, and a haughty spirit before a fall.[19] Better to be of a humble spirit with the lowly, than to divide the spoil with the proud.*

Schlocky work ethic. Proverbs 22:29 (CEV). *If you do your job well, you will work for a ruler and never be a slave.*

Becoming a surety for another person's debt. Proverbs 22:26-27 (CEV*). Don't guarantee to pay someone else's debt. If you don't have the money, you might lose your bed.*

Refusing to be a generous giver. Proverbs 11:25 (CEV). *Generosity will be rewarded: Give a cup of water, and you will receive a cup of water in return.*

Lack of contentment. Hebrews 13:5 (AMP), emphasis added. Let your character [your moral essence, your inner nature] be free from the love of money [shun greed—be financially ethical], being **content** with what you have; for He has said, "I WILL NEVER [under any circumstances] DESERT YOU [nor give you up nor leave you without support, nor will I in any degree leave you helpless], NOR WILL I FORSAKE or LET YOU DOWN or RELAX MY HOLD ON YOU [assuredly not]!"

Addiction to pleasure. Proverbs 21:17 (ESV). Whoever loves pleasure will be a poor man; he who loves wine and oil will not be rich.

Neglecting to save. Proverbs 21:20. *There is desirable treasure, and oil in the dwelling of the wise, but a foolish man squanders it.* God loves it when His children save their money instead of squandering it. Here is a lesson from nature in Proverbs 6:6-8. *Go to the ant, you sluggard! Consider her ways and be wise, Which, having no* *captain, overseer or ruler, provides her supplies in the summer, and gathers her food in the harvest.* At the end of the day it's all God's money anyway so spend wisely, and save often. Be a good steward of His money.

Ignoring instruction. Proverbs 13:18 (ESV). *Poverty and disgrace come to him who ignores instruction, but whoever heeds reproof is honored.*

Overworking to be rich. Proverbs 23:4-5. *Do not overwork to be rich; because of your own understanding, cease! Will you set your eyes on that which is not? For riches certainly make themselves wings; they fly away like an eagle toward heaven.*

Drunkenness and gluttony. Proverbs 23:21a. *For the drunkard and the glutton will come to poverty and drowsiness will clothe a man in rags.*

Refusing to give to the poor. Proverbs 28:27. *He who gives to the poor will not lack. But he who hides his eyes will have many curses.* Make sure to listen to God and give only as He directs. Give generously but give wisely.

Seeking significance through tangible assets. Luke 18:18-23. *Now a certain ruler asked Him, saying, "Good Teacher, what shall I do to inherit eternal life?"*

> *[19] So Jesus said to him, "Why do you call Me good? No one is good but One, that is, God. [20] You know the commandments: 'Do not commit adultery,' 'Do not murder,' 'Do not steal,' 'Do not bear false witness,' 'Honor your father and your mother.' "*
>
> *[21] And he said, "All these things I have kept from my youth."*
>
> *[22] So when Jesus heard these things, He said to him, "You still lack one thing. Sell all that you have and distribute to the poor, and you will have treasure in heaven; and come, follow Me."*

²³ But when he heard this, he became very sorrowful, for he was very rich.

Perhaps this man looked to his wealth as his source of significance and in this way made money his god. Jesus could look into his heart to see his true motivation.

God is our only true source of significance. We are significant only because of what He says about us.

Believing the significancy lie that says, "I am significant when I have _____" (Name the thing such as an amount of money, land, car, house, etc., or a position.) When we seek our identity, value, or validation through the things we own we sin. We are only truly validated, valued, and significant because of what God thinks about us.

Believing the significancy lie that says, "I am significant when I am working." We are not "human doings," we are "human beings" and when God calls us to be still and worship Him, or when He tells us to spend more quality time with our spouse and children we better heed His instructions. It's good to be a hard worker but we need proper balance between work and rest.

MAKE THIS DECLARATION:
"In Jesus' Name, I command all the resulting curses of these ancestral sins and iniquities coming against me to be halted at the cross of Christ."

Now go back over the list and confess and repent of any of these sins that you have personally committed.

(Have a prayer minister pull up the iniquity of the above sins.)

Chapter Four

THE SPIRIT OF MAMMON

Jesus said,
No one can serve two masters; for either he will hate the
one and love the other, or else he will be loyal to the
one and despise the other. You cannot serve God and
mammon. *Therefore I say to you, do not worry about*
your life, what you will eat or what you will drink; nor
about your body, what you will put on. Is not life more
than food and the body more than clothing? Look at the
birds of the air, for they neither sow nor reap nor gather
into barns; yet your heavenly Father feeds them. Are you
not of more value than they? Which of you by worrying
can add one cubit to his stature? (Matthew 6:24-27, emphasis added).

THE WORD "MAMMON" IS USED FOUR TIMES IN THE BIBLE, including the above passage and Luke 16:9, Luke 16:11, and Luke 16:13. It comes from the Chaldean or Aramaic language and it means treasure, riches, or wealth. The word "mam-mon" in the Greek New Testament is actually the word *mammon* so this word is what we call a transliteration. Jesus personified it as an enemy of God. I believe that the word *mammon* is different than money. The New Testament uses five different words that mean money and *argurion is* the most frequently used, occurring in 12 different locations. For example, Paul used the word *argurion* in the well-known passage in I Timothy 6:10 where we read, *For the love of money is a root of all kinds of evil, for which some have strayed from the faith in their greediness, and pierced themselves through with many sorrows.* However, with *mammon* there is an evil spirit behind it that tempts us to trust in our riches, our bank account, and our possessions above trusting in God. That's why Jesus says we can't serve God and mammon at the same time because we make mammon our God.

The spirit of *mammon* causes fear and it always says to you that you don't have enough money or wealth. It will lie to you repeatedly that you don't have enough, no matter how much wealth you amass. Keep in mind that money, *argurion*, is not inherently evil—it is a helpful instrument for exchanging goods and services. However, the spirit of *mammon* is inherently evil.

Mammon seeks to convince us that if we have a certain amount of money, or a certain amount of land, or that the house is paid off, or we must amass a certain amount in our 401k and then we will be secure. The truth is that there is no such thing as security in earthly possessions. That type of security is only an illusion because all worldly possessions can slip through our fingers in a heartbeat. Real and lasting security only comes from God.

Some people think that if they only had x amount of dollars then they would be truly happy. That's a lie because many of the wealthiest persons are also some of the most fearful people. They fear losing all they have worked so hard to collect. *Mammon* will tell you that you don't have enough riches no matter how much you save.

The spirit of *mammon* will persuade you that riches are the answer to your problems. No. God is the answer to your problems. *Mammon* will say, "If I had x amount of wealth then I would be somebody." No, that is the sin of seeking significancy from some other source rather than God.

> *Jesus also said,*
> *Do not lay up for yourselves treasures on earth, where moth and rust destroy and where thieves break in and steal;* [20] *but lay up for yourselves treasures in heaven, where neither moth nor rust destroys and where thieves*

do not break in and steal. [21] *For where your treasure is,
there your heart will be also* (Matthew 6:19-21).

So let me ask you quite bluntly, "Where is your treasure?"
Where is your heart? You can't put your trust in both God and
money for your happiness, security, identity, or comfort. Jesus makes
it crystal clear that it will either be God or *mammon*.

PRAYER OF RELEASE FROM THE SPIRIT OF MAMMON

"Heavenly Father, I confess and renounce the sin of trusting in
money above trusting in You. Lord, I confess and renounce the sin
of coming into agreement with the spirit of fear over not having
enough money saved and the fear of losing my money. I confess and
renounce the sin of looking to my bank account as the source of my
security and happiness. I confess and renounce the sin of gaining my
significance through my net worth and income. I confess and renounce the sin of looking to money as the answer to my problems. I
confess and repent of my sin and the sins of my ancestors for choosing to serve *mammon* over choosing to serve You. I renounce all
agreements that my ancestors and I made with *mammon* by using
money in sinful ways. I confess and repent for me and my ancestors
for being double-minded in the use of money and I choose to seek
first the Kingdom of God. I reject, renounce, and break all agreements with the spirit of *mammon*.

Righteous Judge of the Universe, I humbly come before You
and ask You to remove the spirit of *mammon,* the iniquity of *mammon*, and all the related curses from me and my family to a thousand
generations forward, in Jesus' Name, Amen."

THE CURSE OF PROSPERITY

Somewhat related to the spirit of mammon is the curse of prosperity. Not only do many poor people need financial healing, so also
do many of the rich, but for the rich the pendulum swings the other

way. It's not that they're struggling to live paycheck to paycheck, it's that the focus of their life has shifted off God and family.

I heard about a young man launching a new business and he told his pastor that he had committed to tithe and asked for the pastor to pray for God's blessing on his business endeavor. The business started to take off and the young man held true to his commitment to give the Lord the first of his increase. He became one of the top donors in the church. But as his business continued to develop it became more and more difficult for him to give his tithe because by this time it amounted to a great sum of money.

Eventually he contacted the pastor and said, "I made six million dollars last year. I can't afford to give God six hundred thousand dollars. What can I do?" The pastor replied, "Maybe I need to pray that God shrinks your profits down to where you can afford to tithe again." The young businessman got the point and started tithing again. Sadly, this story demonstrates what happens to many Christian people after God blesses them financially. Our wealth, our stuff, crowds God out of our heart so that He no longer occupies first place.

The Apostle Paul exhorted Timothy to beware of teachers who use "godliness" as a means of gain. In 1 Timothy 6:5b we read, *who suppose that godliness is a means of gain. From such withdraw yourself.* Please don't use the teaching in this book as a type of gimmick or a scheme to get rich because your wealth may become a curse to you.

The writer of Proverbs said,

> *Remove falsehood and lies far from me; give me neither poverty nor riches—feed me with the food allotted to me;* [9] *lest I be full and deny You, and say,*

> *"Who is the LORD?" or lest I be poor and steal, and profane the name of my God* (Prov. 30:8-9).

Loving God and growing in grace and the wisdom and knowledge of the Lord are more important than money. Money is a fleeting thing that's of use for this brief life but no longer. It's better to have a little money but be right with God than to have a lot of money and be far from Him.

PRAYER OF RELEASE FROM THE
CURSE OF PROSPERITY

"Lord, I agree with You that I must seek Your Kingdom and Your righteousness above worldly riches, that money is fleeting while You are eternal. I confess and renounce the curse of prosperity in my life and in the lives of my generational line, in Jesus' Name."

Chapter Five
FREEDOM FROM FINANCIAL WORD CURSES

A. Word Curses Spoken Against You By Others

There are spoken curses from others that can hold power over us. The Bible declares that,

> *Death and life are in the power of the tongue, and those who love it will eat its fruit* (Proverbs 18:21).

Negative words spoken over you by someone in authority have especially strong weight. Here are some examples of word curses that could affect your finances: "You'll never amount to anything." "You're a loser just like your _____." "You'll never get ahead." "You'll always be poor." "You can't get anything right." "No one will ever hire you." "You'll always struggle financially." "You can't handle money." "You are not worth what I'm paying you." "You're going to lose everything."

Ask the Holy Spirit to bring to your remembrance any negative words spoken over you that might affect your finances. List them here:

1) _____

2) _____

3) _____

4) _____

5) _____

PRAYERS TO BREAK WORD CURSES

"I reject, renounce and break all agreements with these words. I cast these words down to the ground and cancel their assignments against me. Any demon assigned to enforce these words I reassign you to dry places now, in the Name of Jesus. Lord, I ask you to flush out of my heart the poison of these words and heal any wounds that they caused, in Jesus' Name, Amen."

B. Negative Words That You Have Spoken Over Yourself

Negative words that you have spoken over yourself also release demonic power. Ask the Holy Spirit to remind you of any destructive words you ever spoke over yourself regarding finances.

List them here:

1) _____

2) _____

3) _____

Then confess and repent, naming the specific negative words spoken by you against yourself. Say, "I agree with You Lord that it was wrong for me to say these negative words over myself and I repent. I reject, I renounce, and I break all agreements with these words. I cast them down to the ground and I declare they no longer have any power over me. Any demon assigned to me to enforce these words I reassign to dry places now, in the Name of Jesus."

C. Witchcraft Curses

Witches are very diligent to send curses against Christians, especially Christian leaders and their families. One major factor in many divorces is financial shortage. According to Proverbs 26:2, if there is any cause whatsoever a curse may alight. The cause can even be generational sin that has never been dealt with. *Like a flitting sparrow, like a flying swallow, so a curse without cause shall not alight* (Proverbs 26:2).

Some Christians protest when I teach that curses can negatively affect us. They like to quote Galatians 3:13 where is it says, *Christ has redeemed us from the curse of the law, having become a curse for us (for it is written, "Cursed is everyone who hangs on a tree")*. They argue that Jesus was made a curse for us so we don't have to concern ourselves with curses coming against us. What they fail to do is read the following verse were it reads, *that the blessing of Abraham might come upon the Gentiles in Christ Jesus, that we might receive the promise of the Spirit through faith* (v.14).

Nothing is automatic when it comes to the finished work of Christ, otherwise, everyone would automatically be saved because Jesus died for all. No, we have to receive Him by faith and in this manner we execute the finished work of Christ on the cross and resurrection and we become a new creation. The same holds true for breaking curses in that we must execute the destruction of curses through faith in Jesus' completed work.

PRAYER TO BREAK WITCHCRAFT CURSES

"In the Name of Jesus, I take authority over all hexes, vexes, spells, curses, and witchcraft used against my finances. I bind and break their power over me, cancel their assignments, and cast them to the ground. I declare that they no longer have any power over me. Any demons assigned to me through these endeavors I now assign to dry places, in Jesus' Name. I declare that the power of these curses is broken, by the power of the blood of Jesus Christ. I ask You, Abba Father, to cut off any witch or warlock who is cursing me from accessing future powers of darkness and that you save and bless them, in Jesus' Name."

D. Curses on Actual Money Given to You.

Witches can put a curse on actual money given to you and use it as a point of contact. Pray: "In Jesus' Name, I break off any witchcraft curses on my money. Any demons on my money, I command you to leave now, in Jesus' Name."

E. Curses that come by giving to an organization or ministry that is not ordained by God.

We need to give with God-given wisdom. If you have given to an ungodly organization it is a matter of simple confession and repentance to break this curse. Also, you may have given money to someone who said they needed food or shelter and without praying, without using your discernment, without listening to God, you gave out of pity or mercy only to find out later that they spent the money on their drug or alcohol addiction. In this case your sin was not walking in discernment and wisdom. We need to give wisely and as God directs. However, don't get under false condemnation at this point. Sometimes when you have earnestly tried to listen to God but don't get any direction, I suppose it is better to err on the side of generosity than on the side of stinginess. Ask the Holy Spirit to bring to mind any such organizations or individuals.

PRAYER OF REPENTANCE

"Father in heaven, I confess that when I gave money to _____ (list person or organization). I did not give because You directed me to do so but because I was _____ (pressured, manipulated, emotional, felt sorry for them, deceived, etc.) I repent for not listening to You and for relying on my own fleshly wisdom. From this day forward, with Your help, I will give only as the Spirit leads me. Help me to be more sensitive to the Holy Spirit, in Jesus' Name, Amen."

Chapter Six

FINANCIAL HEALING
THROUGH FORGIVENESS

HOLDING UNFORGIVENESS IN YOUR HEART TOWARD ANYONE who has hurt you monetarily can keep you imprisoned in financial bondage because you have given legal rights to the enemy. Let the Holy Spirit bring to your remembrance anyone who lied to you to get your money, cheated you, conned you, gave you false promises or withheld money unethically. Were you scammed in a financial deal that drained your finances? Did someone sell you a car that was defective but covered up the defect so you would buy the car? Were you promised a raise when you completed a project but after the job was completed the boss found an excuse to withhold the raise? Were you fired unjustly? Did a landlord refuse to return your deposit after moving out even though you left the house spotless?

My wife, Ruthie, and I experienced this several times. Once we rented a house and we kept it spotless. I had the yard looking much better than when we first moved in. I always trimmed the bushes, watered and mowed the yard, and planted flowers. When we moved we had given the required notification to our landlord and were expecting to get back all or a major portion of our security deposit. To our dismay the landlord found one little overlooked area in the stove and kept the entire deposit. Ouch! Needless to say we were disappointed because we really needed that money but we had to forgive.

There are many ways in which we can be taken advantage of financially but the question is, have we truly forgiven, from our heart, the parties involved? If not, Jesus said, neither will your Heavenly Father forgive you. See Matthew 6:14-15.

> *For if you forgive men their trespasses, your heavenly Father will also forgive you. [15] But if you do not forgive men their trespasses, neither will your Father forgive your trespasses.*

Unforgiveness provides an opening for the enemy to come in and kill, steal and destroy. To close this door we must forgive from our heart. We must give up the right to get even. If there is any vengeance, it belongs to God and God alone. Filing a lawsuit may be appropriate in some circumstances but if that becomes the course of action make sure it is not motivated by vengeance. It is possible to have a righteous motivation such as attempting to stop the culprit from hurting other innocent people but even then we need to make sure we're not fooling ourselves and that we have truly forgiven from the heart.

Unforgiveness toward those who have used us financially can provide a huge opening for the devil to continue to harass us in this area. We cannot take this subject lightly. Have we truly forgiven to the point that we've let go of the offense?

You may need to forgive your parents because they didn't mentor you properly or prepare you to deal with finances. They didn't give you guidance as to what college to choose, or how to save and manage money, or to interview for a job. You were left on your own to fend for yourself so you had to learn through the school of hard knocks. They didn't provide a good example in dealing with financial affairs.

You may need to forgive an entity such as a corporation for not paying you what you are worth. You may need to forgive an ex-spouse for managing an unjust settlement which created a great financial drain. You may need to forgive the IRS for unjustly auditing your tax return year after year.

You also may need to forgive yourself. Perhaps you made an error in judgment. Maybe you made an unwise financial decision. You may have trusted someone about whom you knew very little and they ended up scamming you. Maybe you made a careless error that got you fired or took a job that wasn't a good match. Whatever the case may be, you must forgive yourself.

Write down the financial injustices the Holy Spirit brings to mind and the people involved that you need to forgive.

_____

_____

_____

_____

_____

_____

A PRAYER FOR FORGIVENESS

PRAY THIS PRAYER:

"Abba Father, I forgive _____ from my heart for all the things he/she did to me. (Tell God what they did.) I let them go free. I lay nothing to their charge. I require nothing of them. I release them into your hands, Father, for you to get justice as You so choose. I forgive them from my heart, just because You always forgive me, in Jesus' Name, Amen." [2]

If you have been relying on your own ability to get out of a financial pit pray, "God, the power to overcome lack and poverty is in You, the One who lives in me. I turn away from my self-effort to overcome lack and poverty, and I embrace the power of the Holy Spirit who lives in me. Abba Father, in Jesus' Name, release the flow of the Holy Spirit out through me, to overcome completely all lack and poverty."

Chapter Seven
VOWS, JUDGMENTS, LIES, AND EXPECTANCIES

MOST CHRISTIANS DON'T KNOW WHAT AN INNER VOW IS. Some vows are good vows. The vows I made to my wife, Ruthie, on my wedding day were good vows because I made them to her and before God and the assembly. But an inner vow is a vow I make to myself to be carried out by my own power and strength. I get in trouble in my Christian walk when I rely on my own ability. See Jeremiah 17:5,

> *Thus says the LORD: "Cursed is the man who trusts in man and makes flesh his strength, whose heart departs from the LORD."*

Inner vows are based on judgments. Somebody hurts us or does something we react strongly against and we judge them. Then we inwardly vow that we will never do that or will never allow that to happen again to us. Judgments activate the impartial law of sowing and reaping - what we sow is what we reap. If I sow judgment I am going to reap judgment. Jesus said, *Judge not that you be not judged.*

Inner vows don't just go away over time. Some inner vows we may have made in early childhood and we have forgotten that we ever made them but they put us on a course of negative consequences. When I see negative fruit that repeatedly manifests in a person's life I know that underneath the bitter fruit there is most likely an inner vow. That vow needs to be broken. The bitter fruit keeps showing up no matter how much effort we expend in trying to change.

Inner vows typically begin with the phrase, "I will never." Keep in mind that most inner vows are not even spoken out loud and that is why it is often difficult to locate them on your own.

Inner vows frequently work like a pendulum. For example, let's say that you were raised in a home where your parents struggled financially, living from paycheck to paycheck, and were often late on paying bills. You hated living under such circumstances so you vowed that when you became an adult you would never struggle financially like your parents. You grow up and you fight to tread water and often get behind on your bills—or the pendulum could swing the opposite direction. You become a workaholic and are never home so that your children grow in an essentially fatherless home. Your wife can't stand the loneliness and she eventually files for divorce. The inner vow gets played out but perhaps not in the same way your parents struggled.

Foundational lies represent another factor that disrupt our lives. People often believe lies that hold them in bondage. The lies I speak of are core lies we believe about God, ourselves and others. The lies about God are things we, as mature Christians, would never believe about God in our heads. But the problem is that when we experience trauma, especially as children, our hearts become fertile soil in which the devil will sow these lies. We don't believe these lies intellectually but the lies are implanted deep in our hearts, so when the rubber meets the road, when facing the challenges of everyday life, we act or react according to what is in our hearts. We need to locate any such lies and uproot them.

As children what we believe about our earthly father gets transferred to our Heavenly Father. If dad didn't provide for your needs it's easy to believe the lie that "God will not provide." If dad didn't mentor you and work with you to guide you in the wise way to manage money then you may believe the lie that "God won't give me the wisdom and guidance in managing my affairs."

The key is first to recognize these lies. Once we see them and the destruction they have caused we must confess to God our sin in believing them. Then we cast down the structure using our authority

in Christ. Say, "Father, I repent for believing the lie that
_____. In Jesus' Name, I reject, re-
nounce and break all agreements with this lie."

Expectancies work in a similar fashion. Let's say you always went
without as a child and eventually you develop an expectancy that
you will always go without. An expectancy is the devil's form of
faith —you draw "lack" to yourself. You put out vibes that tempt
others to underpay you or withhold wages, etc. Or, let's say as a
young person you worked hard babysitting and you only got paid a
dollar an hour. You work odds jobs to earn some extra money and
you get short-changed. Out of these types of experiences you develop an expectancy that you will never get paid what you are worth.
And sure enough, you grow up, get different jobs and no matter
where you go you don't get paid what you are worth. These expectancies slime other people who would not ordinarily act in such a
way. Thus, the expectancy gets repeatedly reinforced.

Here is a list of common inner vows, judgments, lies and expectancies that relate to our finances. Check off any lies you've ever believed, the inner vows you've made and any expectancies you've developed and write down any others the Lord brings to mind.

___I will never be poor like my parents

___I will never struggle finan-cially

___I'm the reason my parents struggled financially

___I'm a failure

___I'll never be a financial drain on my family

___I'll never be a workaholic

___If I just had a better job I would be better off

___I'm a loser

___My worth is in how much money I make

___I will never go without

___What I have will be taken from me

___God doesn't provide

___God won't protect my fi-nances

___My worth is in what I do

___I'll never be paid what I'm worth

___Budgets are too hard to keep

___I'll never be able to save money

___I will never live by a budget

___I'll never be deprived of what I want

___I'll never be lazy

___I'll never spend more than I make

___Society owes me a living

___You only live once so spend it while you have it

___I'll never get in debt

___I'll never make unwise financial decisions

___I'll never catch a break

___I'll never make poor investments

___I will always be in debt

___I'll never get behind on my bills

___I'm entitled to my fair share

___No matter how hard I work at it I'll always be poor

___I will never get ahead

___God owes me more than what I have now

___My worth is in what I possess

___I will be wealthy no matter what it takes

___Life should be comfortable

___No matter how hard I try I won't succeed

___I'll always be poor

___I will never be dependent on God to sustain me

___I'll never be a poor provider

___I will always make bad financial decisions

___What I earn will be taken from me

___When things are going well something will happen and I'll lose my money

___ _____

___ _____

___ _____

___ _____

___ _____

PRAYER TO BREAK INNER VOWS, JUDGMENTS, LIES AND EXPECTANCIES

"Heavenly Father, I admit that I was wrong in believing these lies and expectancies and for making these judgments and inner vows.

I ask that you bring these to death at the cross of Christ and resurrect in me the ability to see the truth and to walk in your freedom. I renounce these judgments, inner vows, lies and expectancies. I come out of agreement with_____

(Name all that you checked off and any additional ones the Holy Spirit revealed to you.)

In Jesus' Name, I break their power over me and my financial affairs. I declare, in Jesus' Name, that I am free from all these judgments, inner vows, lies and expectancies. Any demons assigned to me through these things I now command you to leave me now, in Jesus' Name."

Chapter Eight

PAUL COX PRAYERS
(Adapted and Used by Permission)

HEAVENLY FATHER, I RECOGNIZE THAT MY MINDSET OF BEING a victim has inhibited my ability to fulfill the call on my life to rule and reign under the Lordship of Jesus Christ. I also declare that the wealth that I am to gain for the purposes of the Kingdom of God has been stopped up by my ancestors' sin of wanting personal wealth to use for their own purposes. I now declare that I will receive all the wealth that the Lord wants me to have to fulfill my Kingdom mandate of ruling and reigning. Lord, please release all restrictions against the resources that you originally intended for me to have.

Lord, please release me from any ungodly contracts that my ancestors or I agreed to and entered into that have brought us into the spirit of poverty. I pray that You would redeem what the devil has taken away and restore to me and my family Your riches and Your glory.

Lord, I repent for and renounce all generational curses that come with seeking worldly riches. Lord please restore me to seek riches in You alone. I repent for myself and my family line for robbing the poor, swindling, gambling, cheating and using witchcraft to gain wealth. Father, I repent for myself and my generational line for being greedy to gain wealth, power, knowledge, titles, position, mantles, and wisdom from any source other than from You.

I repent for my family line and me that we have not treated and valued the Kingdom of Heaven as we should and that we have exchanged the value of the Kingdom of Heaven for the desires of the heart in the form of an earthly Kingdom. Lord, I repent for both me and my family line for worrying about life, food, and clothing. I repent for me and my family line for laying up treasures on earth where moths and rust destroy and where thieves break in and steal. I repent for me and my family line for robbing You, Lord, and not freely and cheerfully giving our offerings to You out of a heart of love.

I repent for me and my family line for making money our defender, security, and protection.

I repent for believing that chants, spells, fate, superstition, and luck will provide the money we need.

I repent for me and my family line for making money, not You, Lord, the center of the universe.

I repent for me and my family line for not exercising our responsibility to pay money that was owed to governmental agencies. I confess the sin of defrauding, cheating, lying, and stealing from the government. I confess the sin of a begrudging and bitter attitude in paying my taxes. I repent for not recognizing Your anointing on government to provide for the basic necessities of our corporate life. I confess the sin in both me and my family line of criticizing, complaining, and cursing my government for not providing enough for the people.

I confess my sin and the sins of my ancestors of seeking, accepting, treasuring, profiting from, and spending blood money. I also repent for me and my ancestors for adding blood money to our children's inheritance.

I confess the sins of those in my generational line for abandoning and sacrificing family and relationships, land, culture, and even faith in God to seek gold and earthly treasures. I choose to seek after the ultimate treasure of my Lord Jesus Christ with all my heart.

I declare that Jesus came to give us abundant life. Father, in Your mercy, please free me and my future generations of the consequences of a poverty mindset. I repent and confess the lie that godliness implies poverty, lacking in basic necessities, living in poverty, always being in need, and that the children will never procure their education.

I repent for spending money on that which does not satisfy and for not coming to God's living waters to drink.

I repent for myself and my family line for not receiving the inheritance that You had for us; and I choose now to receive the inheritance, abundance, and gifts that You have for us. I ask that they will come in such abundance that we will be able to leave an inheritance for our children and grandchildren.

Lord, please disconnect my family line and me from money that was tied to freemasonry, secret societies, secret agendas, covert operations, ungodly funding of churches and institutions and for money tied to the building of ungodly altars and funding prostitutes.

Lord, break off the curse of sowing much and bringing in little, of eating and not having enough, and of earning wages only to put them into a bag of holes.

I repent for myself and my family line for the belief that the gifts of the Holy Spirit could be purchased or sold. I break the curse that money in my generational line and in my life will perish with me.

Lord, I repent for only seeing me, my needs and wants, instead of seeing You, God, and the needs of others. I repent for lavishly adorning myself while not covering the naked and the poor.

Lord, I repent for making my giving an obligation to You and not a free act of my love. Lord remove the canopy of law and the canopy and yoke of obligation from me. Lord allow me to live in Your grace and Your provision.

I ask You, Holy Spirit, to be the One who directs me in what to give. Lord, make my giving come from an attitude of gratitude and love. I choose to seek and follow Your guidance in my giving.

I break off all generational iniquity that has come against my creativity, my ability to produce and reproduce, my need for food and shelter, the work of my hands, and the capital I have invested.

Lord, I repent for myself and for those in my generational line for seeking fortune, wealth, health, and prosperity using evil forces and powers. I repent for myself and those in my generational line for worshipping false gods for the purpose of prosperity.

I repent for myself and for those in my generational line for any misuse and manipulation of the prophetic gifts for self-gain and for following the ways of Balaam.

I repent for myself and for those in my generational line for discrediting You because we relied on our own prosperity, strength, and abilities, and we assumed we lacked nothing.

Lord, help me to see money with spiritual eyes, knowing it is Your resource and belongs to You.[3]

Lord, I repent for myself and my ancestors for coming into agreement with Satan and seeking riches at all costs and lusting after our own glory, wealth and position at the expense of others and future generations.

I repent for myself and my family line for receiving and agreeing with the sounds, words, and songs of Satan and asking him to make us rich and famous no matter the cost. I repent for lusting after my own glory on this side of eternity, instead of waiting on God to justly, generously, graciously and extravagantly care for and reward me in this life and the next.

I repent and renounce for my ancestors illegally trading future generation's inheritance and blessing for their own immediate gratification and for not having faith in the King of kings to provide for them. I ask You, Lord, to cancel the obligation that my ancestors put on me to pay back what is owed for future trading in the past.

Lord, break off of me the consequences of my family line trading the blessings of future generations for instant gratification. I appeal to Your justice and Your blood shed on the cross, and I ask You to declare in Your heavenly court that the agreements are illegal, null and void.

Lord, please unearth the treasures of darkness stolen from my generational line and from the kingdom of God. Lord, please remove the ungodly guardians over the ungodly places in the depths that hold back what belongs to me and to Your kingdom.

Lord, right now I appeal to Your written word and to the spiritual laws that You have set up in Your kingdom, Your kingdom laws. Where the King's law rules, there will be a year of Jubilee. Lord, since You honored that law thousands of years ago, I declare there has been multiple jubilees.

Lord right now, in my family line, I lay claim for all jubilees, and I declare that today is my Day of Jubilee. I declare that all ungodly trading of the past by my ancestors, and the debt that I have been paying, to become null and void; it is cancelled and is no more. I ask for a seven-fold return at current market price for all that has been lost, stolen, or given away in my generational line. (The above quotes are from the book Generational Deliverance, 2015 Edition. For more information go to aslansplace.com.)

PRAYER TO RELEASE THE
TREASURES OF DARKNESS

Lord, I repent for myself and my ancestors for coming into agreement with Satan and seeking riches at all costs and lusting after our own glory, wealth and position at the expense of others and future generations.

I repent for myself and my family line for receiving and agreeing with the sounds, words, and songs of Satan and asking him to make us rich and famous no matter the cost. I repent for lusting after my own glory on this side of eternity, instead of waiting on God to justly, generously, graciously and extravagantly care for and reward me in this life and the next.

I repent for myself and my family line for manipulating sound and words in order to make us look good and come out on top at all costs. I repent for puffing myself up, instead of seeking to lay down my life for others. I repent for stealing God's glory, proclaiming myself to be a self-made ruler instead of rightfully honoring God alone as the only King of all kings.

I repent for myself and my ancestors for wanting to be the center of the universe and having everyone look and pay attention to me, instead of praising, honoring and giving glory to God, the only wise and true King of kings.

I repent for myself and my family line for trading all that we own and cherish, including parents, siblings, spouse and children in order to receive earthly riches, praise and adoration. I repent for sacrificing my children for riches and promotion and leaving them emotionally starved of parental leadership, protective boundaries, hugs, cuddles and affection that only a parent's love can supply to them. Lord, break the consequences of these actions off of me.

I repent for myself and my family line for passing negative pronouncements, shame, and curse on family and others instead of blessing them. I repent for coming into agreement with the curses and lies of the enemy spoken over me and my family by ungodly leaders, and wolves in sheep's clothing. I ask You, Lord, to break off of me and my generational line those curses, shame, and victimization. I repent for receiving my identity from man, and what others think of me instead of from You, Lord.

I repent for only seeing me, my needs and wants, instead of seeing You, God, and the needs of others. I repent for lavishly adorning myself while not covering the naked and caring for the homeless.

I repent for not guarding my heart or rightly discerning my emotions and responding in the soul rather than in the spirit. I ask You, God to be King over all that I think and feel. I repent for not asking You to seal and protect me, and to close off entrances to the enemy.

I repent for not honoring Your wisdom, Your creation, Your design at an atomic and subatomic level, so that Your glory could come forth and Your light could be seen through me before conception and up until now. I repent for not correctly stewarding God's creation and having godly dominion over the earth instead of greedily abusing God's resources.

I repent for myself and my generational line for coming into agreement with the spirit of greed and worshipping mammon instead of You. I repent for desiring the power and control that money brings and not submitting to Your control, Father God. I repent for desiring Your blessings, but not wanting to position myself in You to be blessed and a blessing to others. Lord, I repent of the greed of my ancestors that gave away my inheritance. I repent for their lies, avarice, greed, and for stealing from future generations.

I repent and renounce for my ancestors illegally trading future generation's inheritance and blessing for their own immediate gratification and for not having faith in the King of kings to provide for them. I ask You, Lord, to cancel the obligation that my ancestors put on me to pay back what is owed for future trading in the past.

Lord, break off of me the consequences of my family line trading the blessings of future generations for instant gratification. I appeal to Your justice and Your blood shed on the cross, and I ask You to declare in Your heavenly court that the agreements are illegal, null and void.

I repent for myself and my ancestors for loving money more than You, Lord, and clinging to the things of this world. I break agreements with the love of money, and let go of the things of this world. I ask You, Lord, to cut off the ungodly strings to wealth.

I pledge my love to You, Jehovah Jireh, and I look to You for provision. I declare that You are the Great I Am and the source of all that I have, all that I am, and all that I am to become. You are my Lord and my Redeemer.

Lord I pray the prayer Abraham Lincoln prayed: "We have forgotten You, Lord. We have forgotten the gracious hand which preserved us in peace and multiplied and enriched and strengthened us, and we have vainly imagined, in the deceitfulness of our hearts, that all these blessings were produced by some superior wisdom and virtue of our own. Intoxicated with unbroken success, we have become too self-sufficient to feel the necessity of redeeming and preserving grace, too proud to pray to the God that made us." Lord, I repent for pride, self-sufficiency, and not giving thanks for the abundant blessings You have given to me.

I repent and renounce for myself and my ancestors for valuing time and my schedule more than You, Lord. I repent for loving time and the control of time, "me" time, my time, quality time, instead of getting into Your time, God, and asking You to order my day according to Your desire. Please forgive me for allowing time to control me, for not seeking You first, or Your rest and restoration. Lord, please release me from any ungodly time warps, or places where I've been stuck in time.

Lord, reestablish my generational timeline according to Your Kairos timeline. Please reconcile me to Your correct Kairos timeline. Lord, remove me from any ungodly timeline that the enemy has placed me on that may be in the depth.

Lord, please purify my time with Your living water. Wash away all the old timelines. Lord, align my inner clock to synchronize with Your heartbeat, sound and movement.

Lord, please cleanse the elements of my physical body and the body of Christ. I declare that I will be a living stone properly fitted together in the body of Christ in timeless eternity with You, Lord.

Lord, please return to my DNA, all components that were given away or stolen from my ancestor's line. Lord, please correctly align the order and sequence of all the components of my DNA. Lord, please restore the health, wealth, blessing, and favor that should be inherent in my DNA structure. Lord, please reverse the curse on my DNA when Adam sinned and return to me the original blessing that was designed in my family's DNA. Lord, release all the inherent blessings that were given to my family's DNA.

Lord, release the components of my DNA that were trapped by the stealing and illegal trading and giving away of my ancestors with the enemy for instant gratification. Lord, reestablish, the vibration of the electrons that connect the elemental parts of my DNA. Reestablish the correct frequency and vibration to the chemical bonds in my DNA.

Lord, please remove me from ungodly places in the heavens, the depth, the length, the width, and the height. Lord, I declare that all the earth belongs to You, and please reestablish the correct grid on the earth, above the earth, and under the earth.

Lord, please unearth the treasures of darkness stolen from my generational line and from the kingdom of God. Lord, please remove the ungodly guardians over the ungodly places in the depths that hold back what belongs to me and to Your kingdom.

Lord, right now I appeal to Your written word and to the spiritual laws that You have set up in Your kingdom, Your kingdom laws. Where the King's law rules, there will be a year of Jubilee. Lord, since You honored that law thousands of years ago, I declare there has been multiple jubilees.

Lord right now, in my family line, I lay claim for all jubilees, and I declare that today is my Day of Jubilee. I declare that all ungodly trading of the past by my ancestors, and the debt that I have been paying, to become null and void; it is cancelled and is no more. I ask for a seven-fold return at current market price for all that has been lost, stolen, or given away in my generational line.

Lord, I anticipate through faith, and declare that my trading will now be done in faith. My trust is in You Lord. Lord, I trade by faith and say You have my life. I trust in You, and I thank You Lord that it will be accomplished according to Your time.

Lord, I present this prayer before You in the heavenly court as the prayer of my heart. I ask You to appropriate this prayer to my own personal life. Lord, I ask for Your justice. I ask that You will render this prayer into Your courts as a legal document. Jesus, as my advocate, I ask that You go before the Father, and ask the Father to declare this a "done deal" in my life and in my generational line.

The above prayers are from the book Generational Deliverance, 2015 Edition, by Paul L. Cox. Copyright©2015. For more information go to aslansplace.com.)

Chapter Nine

CONTENTMENT

THERE IS A STORY ABOUT THE WEALTHY WILLIAM RANDOLPH Hearst who years ago invested a fortune in collecting art treasures from around the world. One day Hearst was reading a description of a valuable art item and he sent his agent abroad to find it. After months of searching, the agent reported that he had finally found the treasure. To the surprise of Hearst, the priceless masterpiece was stored in none other than his own warehouse. The multi-millionaire had been searching all over the world for a treasure he already possessed. Had he read the catalog of his treasures, he would have saved himself a lot of time and money. (From Today in the Word, Dec 13, 1995, pg.20) I think we as believers are like that. Happiness isn't something that's out there some place, that the world can give us, but that Christ has already given us.

The Apostle Paul made a startling statement in Phil. 4:11,

Not that I speak in regard to need, for I have learned in whatever state I am, to be content.

How can a man in prison say such a thing? Here is the man that had received 39 stripes on five different occasions. Three different times he was beaten with rods, once he was stoned, three times he suffered shipwreck, a night and a day he spent in the water and he had gone hungry, all for the sake of the gospel. And yet he said he learned how to be content no matter what the circumstances.

I know very few people I would describe as content. It seems to me that we live in a society where people are searching for peace and contentment but people are looking for it in all kinds of places. The advertising world tries to capitalize on this need by saying, "If you buy this item you will be content or happy or have peace of mind." Or they try to tell you that you need this experience such as a cruise, trip to Europe, or fine dining in Dubai, that happiness is right around the corner.

The question is what is contentment? The Greek word means to be independent of outward circumstances, a sense of satisfaction that is independent of outward circumstances. I like Bill Gothard's definition: "Realizing that God has already provided all I need for my present happiness."

People want to be happy. Happiness is a universal search that crosses all boundaries. But when trouble hits, most people fall apart wondering how they'll survive. Our problem is that most of us look for happiness in people, places or things. As far as I can tell just about every sin people commit can be traced back to a lack of contentment. Think about it! The commandments to not commit adultery, kill, steal, bear false witness and covet would be kept if we learned contentment.

The devil knows this, so how does he tempt us to sin? He tries to get us discontented. Look at Adam and Eve. How could he tempt them? There weren't any other women for Adam to lust after. There weren't other people for them to kill. There was no need to steal because they had it all. There wasn't any Sabbath day to break. There wasn't a neighbor for them to covet his stuff.

I don't know how many different kinds of fruit trees there were in the Garden of Eden but let's say there were a thousand. Now if the devil had said to Eve, "You have 999 trees to eat of but this one you can't eat." If he had put it that way he wouldn't have been able to deceive her. But he asked her, *Has God indeed said, 'You shall not eat of every tree of the garden'?* (Genesis 3:1) You see, he wanted her to focus on the one thing she couldn't have, not on the 999 things she already had.

King David had a harem of women but one night he looked over his balcony and beheld a beautiful woman bathing. She was the wife of another man. He had to have her at any cost. It wasn't that his hormones driving him couldn't be satisfied righteously, that wasn't the issue, it was an issue of discontentment.

Some people might say, "What's so bad about lack of contentment? It causes growth, new inventions like electric light and the telephone, expansion of knowledge, and new conveniences." After all, David caused some good changes in Israel. He expanded his kingdom from 6,000 sq. miles to 60,000 sq. miles. He rid the land of the Philistine threat, established trade routes, built a powerful military, and rid the country of idol worship.

People misunderstand the word contentment. They think it means that you should not pursue anything else, accomplish excellence, or possess more than you have now. They think, "Well the Bible says I'm to be content so I'll just relax, kick back and be lazy." No, contentment means that you're happy **in** your circumstances, not that you're happy **with** your circumstances. We have trouble distinguishing between contentment and apathy. We need to realize that God has provided all our needs for our present happiness.

Look at Hebrews 13:5. *Let your conduct be without covetousness; be content with such things as you have. For He Himself has said, "I will never leave you not forsake you.* Notice he contrasts contentment with covetousness. The opposite of contentment is covetousness. So if we want to learn how to be content we have to deal with covetousness.

In all the years I have been in ministry only one time have I had someone come to me and say, "Pastor, I need prayer, I have a problem with covetousness." The reason is that most people are blinded to it. The old saying goes, "Deceived people don't know they're deceived."

Covetousness is one of the seven deadly sins but most people don't know how deadly it is. *A ruler who lacks understanding is a great oppressor, but he who hates covetousness will prolong his days* (Proverbs 28:16). Covetousness is a form of envy and notice what God says in Proverbs 14:30. *A sound heart is life to the body, but envy is rottenness to the bones.* Do you see how serious it is? It will lead to bone problems and the immune system originates in the bone marrow.

That's why Jesus said,

"Take heed and beware of covetousness, for one's life does not consist in the abundance of the things he possesses"(Luke 12:15).

"Take heed" means to take special note of this one because this one can sneak up on us. And in the same context Jesus said,

For where your treasure is, there your heart will be also (Luke 12:34).

Notice the way He said that. Not where your heart is there your treasure will be. No your heart follows where you put your money. If you invest it into the Kingdom of God, that's where your heart will be.

A typical market in the United States in 1976 stocked 9,000 items; today that same market carries 30,000 different items. And why is that? Because we have an obsessive compulsion to possess more and more things, thinking they will bring satisfaction in our lives. The Old Testament sums it up in the word "covet" which is an unquenchable desire for more. Galatians 5:20 calls it "selfish ambition." The Greek word here literally means "to grasp for more and more." And that's what I'm talking about—that covetous drive for more and more and that desire brings about a lack of contentment. And God takes covetousness very seriously.

Oniomania (oh-nee-uh-MEY-nee-uh) is the psychological term for an uncontrollable desire to buy things. Ask God to deliver you from this behavior. The Holy Spirit indwells every true follower of Jesus Christ. One of the fruits of the Holy Spirit as taught in Galatians 5:22-23 is self-control. He loves to help us with this issue so we don't have to do it on our own by simply setting our will to do it. Here's a prayer that will benefit you in this area: "Holy Spirit, the ability to exercise self-control is in You, the One who lives in me. I ask You to release Your self-control through me, in Jesus' Name,

Amen." And then trust Him to be your Helper. He truly desires to be our Helper in such matters.

Have you ever heard the term "affluenza?" There is a book entitled *Affluenza* by John de Graaf and David Wann that was first published in 2005 that seeks to describe the evils of materialism and consumerism in our culture.[4] De Graff and Wann declare that affluenza is not confined to the rich but affects the poor as well. They assert that this condition contaminates all of us, but in different ways. They go on to say that "the affluenza epidemic" is rooted in the obsessive, almost religious quest for economic expansion that has become the core principle of what is called the American dream.

Our goals seem to be totally out of whack. For example, in America we spend more on shoes, jewelry, and watches than we do on higher education. More Americans have declared personal bankruptcy than have graduated from college. We spend more on automobile maintenance than on religious and charitable organizations. Our annual creation of trash would fill a fleet of garbage trucks stretching halfway to the moon. We have twice as many shopping centers as high schools.

And Americans seem to be driving themselves to an early grave in order to get the money needed to buy all the things they want. Currently Americans work more hours each year than do the citizens of any other industrialized country, including Japan. The Department of Labor statistics say that full-time American workers are putting in 160 hours more per year (essentially one month more) than they did in 1969. And almost all of our workers say they yearn to spend more time with their families.

Many people have the idea, "Get all you can, can all the rest, and sit on the lid." One of the best ways to free yourself from the stranglehold of covetousness is to learn the grace of giving. When I sow money, time and talents into kingdom work I am making a declaration, "God I acknowledge that You are the source of my happiness." The Apostle Paul said in the context of money, *Now godliness with contentment is great gain.*[7] *For we brought nothing into this world, and it is certain we can carry nothing out.*[8] *And having food and clothing, with these we shall be content* (1 Timothy 6:6-8). Possessions do not make us happy and we need to wake up to that truth.

We get attached to our stuff and the best way to wean us away from stuff is to let go of some of it. When that rich young ruler came to Jesus, you know what Jesus told him to do, he told him to sell his possessions and give to the poor. Jesus' advice to the rich young ruler was very practical. If we want contentment we need to learn to let go of the world's goods.

One of the by-products of giving some of it away is that it teaches us that we can get by on less. It teaches us that we don't need those things to be happy. By letting go of our money and some of our conveniences we find that we don't need all that junk to be happy. We can get by on less.

Did you know that the average person in America living at the poverty level is wealthy compared to the majority of the world? And yet we think, if I just had that other job, if I had a home like them, if my mother in law would move out of state, then I would be happy. No, God has already provided everything I need for my present happiness. Paul said, "In whatever state I am, I have learned to be content." This verse means contentment is something that can be learned.

Notice what Paul said in Philippians 4:13 in the Amplified Version. *I have strength for all things in Christ Who empowers me —I am ready for anything and equal to anything through Him Who infuses inner strength into me, [that is, I am self-sufficient in Christ's sufficiency].*

In this verse Paul was saying that his contentment was not in doing but in knowing whose he was. Many people today seek to find satisfaction in doing. Many men in particular find their identity as a person in their jobs. If the job is going well then they are doing fine. Workaholism is one addiction that our culture glorifies but sadly, it destroys families. Paul could have found satisfaction in his work as an apostle first, but it doesn't seem this is the case. Paul didn't have the mentality of many people today because his sufficiency came from Christ.

PRAYER FOR CONTENTMENT

"Heavenly Father, I confess that there have been times when I've lacked contentment and that I've looked to the wrong sources to find it. I confess my sin of covetousness, of wanting more stuff to make me happy. Lord, I repent. From this day forward, with Your help, I will walk in Your freedom. Help me to be like the Apostle Paul and be content in whatever circumstances I find myself. Holy Spirit, circumcise my heart and cut away the discontent and replace it with true contentment, in Jesus' Name, Amen."

Part II

SIGNIFICANCY CURSES

A S STATED EARLIER, MANY OF THE FINANCIAL CURSES GET passed down through the bloodline so that we inherit from our ancestors a susceptibility, a propensity, to experience persistent or reoccurring financial lack. In the book of Judges we discover that the Children of Israel faced seven different enemies that forced them to struggle to survive, to worry about having their basic needs met. These seven enemies are the Arameans, the Moabites, the Philistines, the Canaanites, the Midianites, the Shechemites (Jotham's Curse), and the Ammonites and these enemies consumed the resources of the Israelites. It is important to know that these enemies match up to what I call the significancy curses which affect our lives today.[6]

These seven curses correspond to the seven motivational gifts found in Romans chapter 12 which reads,

> *For as in one body we have many members, and the members do not all have the same function, [5] so we, though many, are one body in Christ, and individually members one of another. [6] Having gifts that differ according to the grace given to us, let us use them: if prophecy, in proportion to our faith; [7] if service, in our serving; the one who teaches, in his teaching; [8] the one who exhorts, in his exhortation; the one who contributes, in generosity; the one who leads, with zeal; the one who does acts of mercy, with cheerfulness* (vss. 4-8, ESV).

I refer to this list of gifts as motivational gifts because they describe our basic motivation, the way we are wired, the way we approach life and the way they flavor the other spiritual gifts we operate in. The seven motivational gifts are prophet, servant, teacher, exhorter, giver, leader (or ruler), and mercy. Each of these gifts has strengths and each also possesses certain weaknesses.

When one of these curses comes into my family line it is because either I or an ancestor let it in through sin. I or my ancestor sinned in a specific way that related to their primary motivational gift.[7] I know this may seem confusing but hang in there and hopefully it will become clear. If the curse is in my generational line only and not the result of my sin, the curse will affect me even though I have a different motivational gift than my ancestor who let the curse into my bloodline. The curse may be the result of my own sin or the sin of my ancestor when I or my ancestor believed a lie related to one's significance. We will go through the list of curses explaining the Biblical backdrop and what activated them. We will trace each one back to its significancy lie and as we do we must confess and repent for believing the corresponding significancy lie. A significancy lie is the lie that says, "I am significant when I _____ " or "I am somebody when I _____" or "I am validated when I _____ ." The truth is I am not valid, I am not valuable, I am not significant because of my particular efforts or accomplishments, I am somebody because of what God says about me. When I look to the wrong source for my validation I allow a curse of the enemy to come in and torment me. Let's take a look at these seven significancy curses.

Chapter Ten

THE ARAMEAN CURSE

And the people of Israel did what was evil in the sight of the LORD. They forgot the LORD their God and served the Baals and the Ashtaroth. ⁸ Therefore the anger of the LORD was kindled against Israel, and he sold them into the hand of Cushan-rishathaim king of Mesopotamia. And the people of Israel served Cushan-rishathaim eight years. ⁹ But when the people of Israel cried out to the LORD, the LORD raised up a deliverer for the people of Israel, who saved them, Othniel the son of Kenaz, Caleb's younger brother. ¹⁰ The Spirit of the LORD was upon him, and he judged Israel. He went out to war, and the LORD gave Cushan-rishathaim king of Mesopotamia into his hand. And his hand prevailed over Cushan-rishathaim. ¹¹ So the land had rest forty years. Then Othniel the son of Kenaz died (Judges 3:7-11, ESV).

NOTICE THAT EVERY ONE OF THESE CURSES CAME INTO THE bloodline through sin. This passage says that they did evil in the sight of the Lord and consequently they could not get justice in an established system. We call this the Aramean Curse. The telltale sign of the Aramean Curse is that you can't get justice in a time-honored structure. Everybody encounters injustices from time to time but the people under this curse experience injustice repeatedly, as a pattern of life. As previously stated, for years my wife, Ruthie, and I rented the homes we lived in. We took diligent care of the inside and outside of the property leaving it in better condition than when we moved in. Without exaggeration, we almost always improved the landscaping, being careful to water, mow, and weed the yard. We would leave the inside spotless before turning over the key to the owner or manager. Invariably, however, they would find some reason to withhold the deposit. Later I had to do some serious exercises in forgiveness for being unjustly treated by these landlords. Little did we know that we operated under an Aramean Curse.

Some years ago I was rear-ended while waiting at a red light and the accident caused some neck issues for which I received many treatments. It was obviously not my fault but the insurance settlement was unjust paying only a fraction of the medical costs. Another time a hail storm came through our neighborhood. Nearly everyone else in our cul-de-sac had their roofs replaced by their insurance companies so I thought I better get my roof inspected. Two different roofing companies confirmed that there was significant damage to the roof as well as collateral damage. Our insurance company fought it and eventually paid us a whopping $151.00 to replace our roof! That's injustice. Some people have this type of thing happen all the time. Some people repeatedly get unjust treatment by the IRS, being audited year after year, or are not allowed to get their 501(c)3 status for their non-profit organization. Or they may have a very slight fender bender making a tiny little scratch but the other driver takes them to small claims court and wins a settlement of $1,800. There are a million ways this curse can get played out but every time the individual appeals for justice they cannot get it.

Now go back to the above Scripture passage and notice the two names. The first is of the king, "Cushan-Rishathaim," and the second one is the name of the land, "Aram Naharaim." The entire region was known as Aram. Aram Naharaim speaks of a city or a land where there are two rivers. In the natural, two rivers flow there but there is also a spiritual application. "Cushan" means "their darkness," inferring that this individual was evil and was evil because of generational heritage. However, he was not just a bad person, he was a really bad person. "Rishathaim" speaks of a doubling of the evil, a pro-liferation of evil. But what was so evil about what he had done?

Now go back to the idea of two rivers and put aside the notion of a natural, physical river flowing with water and consider the fact that God has designed, that in every community or social grouping, there are to be the existence of a political river and a spiritual river. Read through the Old Testament and notice the relationship be-tween kings and priests. The priestly role was separate from the king-ly role. Kings were not allowed to offer sacrifices, they were not al-lowed to go into the holy of holies, but at the same time, the priests and prophets often took the initiative in speaking into the lives of the kings and in this way directed the course of the nation. Similarly, at the foundation of the USA, in New England, pastors spoke to the political issues before an election. And on the same day as the elec-tion they held a religious service where the newly elected officials would attend. Then the pastor proceeded to lecture those elected politicians on how to run the city government according to God's principles. The pastors didn't control them but they hoped to influ-ence them.

God designed it so these two streams would run closely together, yet separately. Nevertheless, when you look at history you see that many nations experienced the religious stream controlling the politi-cal stream. Quite often the religious stream represented the spiritual dark side, of occultic power, and they used this power to control the political stream. For example, in the Great Britain area centuries ago, the Druidic priests pretty much controlled society. The king or the other royalty did not dare to act contrary to the advice and counsel of the Druid priests. The political arena was merely a puppet of the religious realm. Another example is the Mayans. In their ancient civilization the government was dominated and controlled by the priesthood. Also, a number of Native American tribes had shamans who completely dominated the tribal chief. In this way the political sphere's hands were tied in making fair and just rulings on behalf of the people under them.

So how did it get this way? At some juncture in history the political sphere sold their political authority to the religious realm in order to gain power. The political authority gave his authority to the occultic realm in exchange for power and they empowered him during his lifetime. But once he died the authority of his position as a political ruler remained in the hands of the religious or occultic realm. So all the following generations have to live with the burden of the political power being given to the religious. And that is what Cushan-Rishathaim did. In order for him to gain power and dominion in his lifetime as a king, he traded his legacy of the political realm to the religious and the religious community kept it after his death. Today this dynamic in a country's history leads to them not being able to get justice internationally.

THE SIGNIFICANCY LIE

That's how it affects nations but how does the Aramean Curse get into an individual's generational line? Very simply, one of our ancestors with the motivational gift of prophet encountered a problem that was bigger than he could fix. He was asked to take care of a problem that was beyond his ability and rather than admitting that he couldn't fix it, he decided to team up with the dark side to obtain the power to fix it. If a person's significancy is found in his/her ability to fix things then they fear they have no value or lack significance if they come against a problem they can't fix. A person with the dominate motivational gift of prophet has an anointing and a desire to fix things—it's the way God wired them and it is right and good and proper for them to want to fix things. The trouble comes when they seek to get their identity or significance through successfully fixing problems. That represents a false sense of identity, validity, or value.

When someone in your generational flow, knowingly or unknowingly, tapped into occult power to be able to fix problems that they couldn't fix by using their own skill set or expertise, it causes you to be burdened down with the Aramean Curse. It is important to understand that what your ancestors did is very significant. When they crossed the line and sought forbidden knowledge, that iniquity gets passed down to their children and their children's children for four generations. And your finances get devoured because you can't get justice in matters of business or in the judicial system.

PRAYER TO BREAK THE ARAMEAN CURSE

"Heavenly Father, I declare, in Jesus' Name, that the blood covenant I have with Jesus Christ of Nazareth, the Christ who has come in the flesh, supersedes all other covenants made by me and my ancestors. And because I am in a covenant relationship with the Lord Jesus Christ I have the legal right to be free from the Aramean Curse. Righteous Judge of the universe, I humbly ask You to open the books of my family line and identify every one of my ancestors who operated in the Aramean Curse and please identify every significancy lie that they believed. I confess the sin of my ancestors for trying to fix problems that were not theirs to fix. I confess the sin of my ancestors for failing to fix difficult situations that You called them to fix. I reject, renounce, and break all agreements with the lie that says, "My significancy or validity comes through resolving or fixing problems." I confess the sin of my ancestors who made the choice to use occultic power to resolve problems and I reject, renounce, and break all agreements with those choices. On behalf of my generational line I confess and renounce the sin of serving and worshipping the Baals and the Ashtaroth. I admit to You Lord, that it was just, right, and proper for this curse to come into my generational line. I accept Your justice in permitting the devil to consume my generational line because of these bad choices. But because I am in a covenant relationship with You, because of the finished work of Jesus, Your Son, I have a higher legal right. Because of the blood of Jesus, Your power is available to destroy these curses and I receive the cleansing You promised in Your Word. I send the Aramean Curse in my bloodline to the cross of Christ, in Jesus' Name. And I declare, in Jesus' Name, that this curse is rendered null and void. I declare that, my spouse, my children and I are now cleansed of the Aramean Curse, in Jesus' Name. I command that any and every demon sent to empower this curse are now reassigned to dry places. Leave now and never return, in Jesus' Name. I decree and declare that the Aramean Curse in my life is now broken, in Jesus' Name."

"I ask You Father to release every blessing that has been blocked by the Aramean Curse. Thank You for those blessings that have been accumulated for me in heaven, in Jesus' Name, Amen."

When you shatter the Aramean Curse the appropriate legal system and Godly justice are let loose upon your life and the sphere in which you interact with others.

Chapter Eleven

THE MOABITE CURSE

THIS CURSE POSSIBLY INFLUENCES MORE INDIVIDUALS THAN the other six significancy curses. The Scripture passage for this curse is about king Eglon, the king of Moab, and Ehud, the left-handed judge.

In Judges 3:12-30 we read,

And the people of Israel again did what was evil in the sight of the LORD, and the LORD strengthened Eglon the king of Moab against Israel, because they had done what was evil in the sight of the LORD. ¹³ He gathered to himself the Ammonites and the Amalekites, and went and defeated Israel. And they took possession of the city of palms. ¹⁴ And the people of Israel served Eglon the king of Moab eighteen years.

¹⁵ Then the people of Israel cried out to the LORD, and the LORD raised up for them a deliverer, Ehud, the son of Gera, the Benjaminite, a left-handed man. The people of Israel sent tribute by him to Eglon the king of Moab. ¹⁶ And Ehud made for himself a sword with two edges, a cubit in length, and he bound it on his right thigh under his clothes. ¹⁷ And he presented the tribute to Eglon king of Moab. Now Eglon was a very fat man. ¹⁸ And when Ehud had finished presenting the tribute, he sent away the people who carried the tribute. ¹⁹ But he himself turned back at the idols near Gilgal and said, "I have a secret message for you, O king." And he commanded, "Silence." And all his attendants went out from his presence. [20] And Ehud came to him as he was sitting alone in his cool roof chamber. And Ehud said, "I have a message from God for you." And he arose from his seat. [21] And Ehud reached with his left hand, took the sword from his right thigh, and thrust it into his belly. [22] And the hilt also went in after the blade, and the fat closed over the blade, for he did not pull the sword out of his belly; and the dung came out. [23] Then Ehud went out into the porch and closed the doors of the roof chamber behind him and locked them.

[24] When he had gone, the servants came, and when they saw that the doors of the roof chamber were locked, they thought, "Surely he is relieving himself in the closet of the cool chamber." [25] And they waited till they were embarrassed. But when he still did not open the doors of the roof chamber, they took the key and opened them, and there lay their lord dead on the floor.

[26] Ehud escaped while they delayed, and he passed beyond the idols and escaped to Seirah. [27] When he arrived, he sounded the trumpet in the hill country of Ephraim. Then the people of Israel went down with him from the hill country, and he was their leader. [28] And he said to them, "Follow after me, for the LORD has given your enemies the Moabites into your hand." So they went down after him and seized the fords of the Jordan against the Moabites and did not allow anyone to pass over. [29] And they killed at that time about 10,000 of the Moabites, all strong, able-bodied men; not a man escaped. [30] So Moab was subdued that day under the hand of Israel. And the land had rest for eighty years (ESV).

With the Aramean Curse you lose, through unjust means, your capital that you hold, but with the Moabite Curse the funds don't get to you in the first place. When the Moabite Curse is in play you experience people making promises regarding finances that they don't execute. For example, you get a new job at a startup company at a very low salary and the boss promises that once the company gets up and running you'll get a significant raise, but the raise never happens. With the Moabite Curse your superior promises that once you pay your dues that eventually it will pay off, but it never materializes.

A sign of the Moabite Curse is that you are always having to pay your dues every place you go. Every place you go you have to earn respect by starting out at the bottom and working your way up. In the absence of the Moabite Curse honor accumulates because of your increased work-related knowledge and skill. It doesn't matter what kind of job you hold, blue collar, white collar, if the Moabite Curse is at work you'll find yourself having to pay your dues repetitively, that honor does not build up from past workplace experience and accomplishments.

Another telltale sign of the Moabite Curse is that your boundaries are repeatedly infringed upon. For women under this curse they consistently find that when they get around men their boundaries aren't honored, that men undress them with their eyes, or give a hug that lasts a little too long, or use sexual innuendo.

Another area of the infringement of boundaries is in your personal space. In the workplace there exists an unwritten, unspoken set of rules about valuing other workers' terrain. However, if you regularly experience co-workers walking into your office without knocking, or entering your office when you're not there to help themselves to your stapler or paperclips, to get on your computer, to checking out your address file, etc. They consistently dishonor your personal space in various ways while at the same time respecting the personal space of others. When this happens look for the presence of the Moabite Curse.

Some pastors are very good at setting their personal boundaries. People in their church know their boundaries and honor them. Other churches believe their pastor should be available around the clock if needed and they will drop by their home unannounced to visit anytime, day or night. When I pastored a church in Southern California years ago, I had a church member who literally liked to call on the phone at 11:00 at night and then would turn around and call at 6:00 in the morning. She thought that I was at her beck and call 24/7. Thank God this behavior represented a rarity for me but for pastors under the Moabite Curse this type of activity gets played out repeatedly. One exasperated pastor's wife finally said to her husband, "If the church was a woman I'd snatch her baldheaded." That poor woman probably suffered the effects of her husband being under the Moabite Curse.

The lady that called me night and day was violating my time. Some people don't honor anybody's time and if you're under the Moabite Curse people regularly dishonor your time. They eat up your time with trivial matters. They ask questions for which they could find the answers on their own by doing their own research. They come by your home unannounced to just hang out when you're right in the middle of a crucial project because they have no regard for the value of your time. This represents another indication of the Moabite Curse.

Another indicator of the Moabite Curse involves the pattern of the dishonoring of your personal, private information. Let's say, for example, you share with your intercessors a personal medical issue and you ask them to keep it confidential. You show up at church on Sunday and a half a dozen people ask you about your medical condition—that characterizes a violation of your boundaries regarding private information.

There is another more problematic situation and that is when there are no boundaries or limits to what you are required to give. Go back to the Judges 3 passage and look at verse 18 which reads, *And when Ehud had finished presenting the tribute.* Scripture is full of instances of measurable, definable tribute, which is a fixed amount, but the Israelites were not required to pay tribute to the Moabites. The word "tribute" in this case is an inaccurate translation. Instead of a tribute it was an open-ended amount. Sometimes people demand of us an open-ended amount of time, effort, or money.

The Israelites had to pay enough money as a gift to Moab to keep them from harming them any more than they already had. The Israelites didn't know exactly how much was enough. It would have been much easier for them if they had known the exact amount. To illustrate, let's say you work for a demanding boss who piles on a huge workload. You put in your 40 hours every week working diligently to complete the assigned tasks. But even though you did an excellent job, on your quarterly review the boss dings you for not putting in enough effort and suggests that you put in longer hours. The next quarter you average 50 hours per week only to receive the same complaint. So the next quarter you put in 60 hours per week with the same response. Your frustration lies in the fact that the boss never tells you specifically how many hours are required but always wants more work out of you. That is a marker of the Moabite Curse.

Another and most important way that your boundaries can be violated is when your authorities make your boundaries so small that you can't leave. Go back to the book of Judges and consider the fact that about ten thousand Moabites lived in Israel's borders but the major problem Israel had with them was that the Moabites controlled the amount of people that could come and go. In verse thirteen it says, *And they took possession of the city of palms.* The city of Palms is actually the city of Jericho. Jericho was positioned at a major ford crossing the Jordan River, so the Moabites controlled the highway into Israel and they commanded the flow of international business. Israel has been actively involved in international commerce perhaps since their conception because it is a part of their DNA but when the Moabites took control of this major highway it was devastating. So naturally the Israelites fought to take back control of the fords so that they could come and go and compete in international commerce. How does this historical information apply to us today? Let's say, for example, that your parents, through control and manipulation, didn't allow you and your spouse and kids to move out of the area because this would mean they couldn't have regular contact with their grandkids.

Don't misunderstand, it is good and right and proper for grand-parents to want to have lots of contact and quality time with their grandchildren, but if God has called you to move some place out of the state, that's a different story. The grandparents should not be so selfish and clingy that they refuse to let you live out your God-ordained destiny. When your parents decline to let you follow the call of God, the Moabite Curse will overtake you.

I'll never forget when my 19-year-old son was given an oppor-tunity by his employer to move from our home in the San Francisco Bay Area in California to the Dallas area in Texas, thousands of miles away. He had earnestly prayed about it and felt God was in it. He ran the decision by my wife and me and we gave him our blessing. I hat-ed the idea of his leaving but I knew that he needed the freedom to make his own decisions and, looking back, many years later, I'm so glad we did.

Maybe your parents pressured you to work in the family business when you didn't have the tiniest bit of desire to do so. Or perhaps your parents pushed you to go to their alma mater when you wanted to attend another university, or they pressured you to marry a wom-an whose family would boost their social standing. Or perhaps your pastor refused to release you when you sincerely believed that God had called you to another church. Out of selfishness he wouldn't bless your decision because he wanted to keep the talent in his own church rather than having a kingdom mindset. Or perhaps your em-ployer insists on leaving you to work in a position that is extremely below your skill set level. All of these actions by your authorities point to the presence of the Moabite Curse in your life. These sce-narios represent some indicators that this curse is active but how did this curse originate?

Let's read now in Genesis 19 to see where it all began as we learn about the inception of the Moabite nation. In verses 30-31 we read,

> *Now Lot went up out of Zoar and lived in the hills with his two daughters, for he was afraid to live in Zoar. So he lived in a cave with his two daughters.*[31] *And the*

firstborn said to the younger, "Our father is old, and there is not a man on earth to come in to us after the manner of all the earth (ESV).

The backdrop to this story is that we find that Lot was living in Sodom. Two angels had announced that God was going to destroy five cities including Zoar. One angel warned Lot to get out of Sodom and go to the hills. Lot balked at the thought of going to the hills so he asked if he could go to Zoar instead and that no harm would come to this little city. The angel agreed to let him go there saying, "We'll spare the city for your sake. Escape there quickly." Lot started to flee to Zoar, but when he saw the massive devastation of the other four cities he changed his mind and headed to the hills after all. And he made a cave his home along with his two daughters.

It seems that the trauma of losing his wife, losing most of his wealth, losing his home and familiar surrounding and seeing the utter destruction of four cities had a profound effect on Lot's emotional well being. It's as though he shut down and possibly suffered from what we would call today post traumatic stress disorder. He wasn't able to pull his life back together and to adequately nurture and guide his daughters in finding husbands. For Lot and his daughters to eat they had to have contact with the world around them. There had to have been an exchange of money or goods in order to survive.

The problem was not that they were in an unworkable circumstance. The problem was that Lot shut down emotionally and couldn't or wouldn't fulfill his responsibility to construct a stage for his daughters to thrive as women. Lot was interacting commercially with civilization around him, yet he neglected to look for suitable mates for his daughters. If nothing else it was only about a six to eight hours hike to his uncle Abraham's place where Abraham would have gladly provided the necessities of life while Lot got back on his feet. Perhaps his pride kept him from reaching out to his uncle.

Although the Bible doesn't say, it could be that Lot was motivated by selfish desire. If his daughters married their husbands probably wouldn't like the idea of living in a cave and would take his daughters elsewhere. Or maybe he just wanted to use his daughters as maids to take care of him for the remainder of his life. Whatever his motivation may have been the point is that he didn't construct a stage for his daughters to flourish, but that's not the worst part of the story. So the oldest daughter said to her sister, "Our father is old and there is no man around here."

Beginning in verse 32 the sordid incestuous plan unfolds as the older sister says to the younger,

> *"Come, let us make our father drink wine, and we will lie with him, that we may preserve offspring from our father."* [33] *So they made their father drink wine that night. And the firstborn went in and lay with her father. He did not know when she lay down or when she arose.*
>
> [34] *The next day, the firstborn said to the younger, "Behold, I lay last night with my father. Let us make him drink wine tonight also. Then you go in and lie with him, that we may preserve offspring from our father."* [35] *So they made their father drink wine that night also. And the younger arose and lay with him, and he did not know when she lay down or when she arose.* [36] *Thus both the daughters of Lot became pregnant by their father.* [37] *The firstborn bore a son and called his name Moab. He is the father of the Moabites to this day.* [38] *The younger also bore a son and called his name Ben-ammi. He is the father of the Ammonites to this day* (ESV).

With the Moabite Curse you have an authority who is dishonoring your boundaries. He refuses to construct a stage or a launching pad for you to thrive, to flourish in God's call upon your life, or he will not even allow you to go out on your own. If you have respectfully, in humility, approached your authority about giving his blessing for you to leave and he has refused, and you continue to submit yourself to him for the sake maintaining peace, you put yourself under the Moabite Curse. In such a case, if you submit to his leadership for the sake of keeping the peace rather than walking in your God-ordained destiny, you sin. And this sin causes you to walk in the Moabite Curse.

If you take your freedom the wrong way by disrespecting your authority, by not humbly approaching him and asking for his blessing in you leaving to follow God's direction, you sin. If you stubbornly and defiantly simply walk away, you sin. Lot erred in the way he treated his daughters, but his daughters also did wrong in the way they devised their liberty so the lesson in the story is to take your freedom in a Godly way. The Bible is clear that we are to honor and submit to our parents and other authorities in our lives.

The right way to do it is to appeal to your authority graciously. Beforehand, make sure you have prayed God's blessings upon him. When you know the timing is right make an appointment. Sit down in his office face to face and very quietly, with humility, with carefully chosen words, without blame or accusation, explain your situation. Seek to be a life-giver even if the person is known for his bad temper and has a track record for destroying people who oppose him.

Let's go back to the book of Judges. Notice that God allowed the Moabites to subjugate the Israelites for eighteen long years. When the timing was right God raised up a deliverer, Ehud. For Ehud or any other leader to lead a rebellion against their oppressors at an earlier time would have been wrong. Timing is the critical issue. At the right time God raised up Ehud, he was not self-appointed, and God said, "Now is the time to free yourselves from the Moabites." So when you leave your present authority make sure that God is saying the time is now.

THE SIGNIFICANCY LIE

The significancy lie that motivates the person with the motivational gift of servant to continue in an authoritarian, overbearing environment is, "I am significant when I can construct a launching pad for others to accomplish their dreams." The person with the motivational gift of servant doesn't look for their own fame but they get their significancy out of helping others to realize their goals. It becomes easy for the servant to fall into the rescuer mindset and they feel like a failure when they are unable to help a person walk out their destiny.

And so often servants will stay in an abusive environment where their authority is not releasing them to walk out their destiny. They do this because they hold to the unrealistic expectation that somehow they can guide their leader into freedom and fruitfulness. By developing a savior mentality the servant allows the Moabite Curse to gain a foothold and the iniquity of the curse gets passed on to his or her children and children's children.

Now let's consider the benefits of dismantling the Moabite Curse. Our culture has a difficult time releasing people to walk in God's design for them, but if you really want to be free from the Moabite Curse take a look at Judges 3:30 where we read, *So Moab was subdued that day under the hand of Israel. And the land had rest for eighty years* (ESV). It is important to note that in some cases the Bible doesn't say how long the land had peace after the enemy was defeated. In other cases it says 40 years, but in this instance it specifically states that it was 80 years. With the Moabites God doubled the norm, two generations of peace instead of only one.

I believe God is telling those who are under this curse do whatever you need to do to break it in your life because it will be well worth the struggle. Maybe you have to go against your parents' wishes in taking your freedom, or perhaps you have to lovingly confront your pastor in order to go where God has called you, and the thought of being assertive frightens you. Just remember that great blessings await you. Consider Abraham who was willing to leave his country and family, to go without their blessing to another land. And as God promised blessings to his descendants, remember it's not just about you. It's about your children and grandchildren being free of the Moabite Curse.

PRAYER TO BREAK THE MOABITE CURSE

"Most High God, I rejoice that You have called me to be in a covenant relationship with You. And because of this covenant I have the legal right to be released from the Moabite Curse. Righteous Judge of the universe, I humbly ask You to open the books of my family line and identify every one of my ancestors who operated in the Moabite Curse and please identify every significancy lie they believed. I reject and renounce the lie that says, "I am significant when I am able to construct a launching pad of success under other people." I confess and renounce the sin of my ancestors for failing to construct a launching pad of success for those under their authority and to release them at the proper time.

I ask You, Lord, to identify every circumstance where there was an authority in my family line or in charge of my family line who refused to let go of those who should have been freed to walk out their God-ordained destiny. I confess this as sin because this behavior is opposed to Your design.

I also ask You to identify every occurrence where an ancestor who was under authority chose to keep the peace at the expense of fulfilling their destiny. I confess that that is sin and I renounce that activity.

I ask You, Father, to identify every situation where someone in my bloodline took their liberty in the wrong way trying to live out their destiny. I confess and renounce that as sin.

Lord, cover these sins related to the Moabite Curse with the blood of Jesus Christ, Your Son. I admit to You Lord, that it was just, right, and proper for this curse to come into my generational line because of sin. I accept Your justice in permitting the devil to consume my generational line because of these bad choices. But because I am in a covenant relationship with You, because of the finished work of Jesus, Your Son, I have a higher legal right. Because of the blood of Jesus, Your power is available to destroy this curse and I receive the cleansing You promised in Your Word. I send the Moabite Curse in my life and in my bloodline to the cross of Christ, in Jesus' Name. And I declare, in Jesus' Name, that this curse is rendered null and void. I declare that, my spouse, my children and I are now cleansed of the Moabite Curse, in Jesus' Name. I command that any and every demon sent to empower this curse are now reassigned to dry places. Leave now and never return, in Jesus' Name. I decree and declare that the

Moabite Curse in my life is now broken, in Jesus' Name. I ask You Father to release every blessing that has been blocked by the Moabite Curse. Thank You for those blessings that have been accumulated for us in heaven, in Jesus' Name, Amen."

When the Moabite Curse is broken we are empowered to establish proper boundaries and proper avenues to help us expand our boundaries.

Chapter Twelve
THE PHILISTINE CURSE

T HE THIRD OF THE SEVEN SIGNIFICANCY CURSES IS THE PHILISTINE
Curse and it corresponds to the gift of teaching, the third motivational gift listed in Romans chapter twelve. This curse seeks to
hinder Jesus Christ from taking the position of Lord or King of the
land. The book of Judges references the Philistines two times. The
first passage is very brief but warrants our attention. It simply reads,

> *After him was Shamgar the son of Anath, who killed six*
> *hundred men of the Philistines with an ox goad; and he*
> *also delivered Israel* (Judges 3:31).

He defeated a large contingent of Philistines, 600 in fact, with
just an ox goad! An ox goad was a long stick with a pointed end used
for prodding animals. It could be up to ten feet long with an iron
spear on one end and a flattened piece of metal on the other. Thus, it
was a formidable weapon in the hands of a skilled fighter but it
demonstrated a unique weapon to defeat a group this large.

God likes to use atypical means to shatter the Philistine Curse and
this is because God wants to display His power over our most dread-
ful enemies. In Colossians 2:15 we read, *Having disarmed principalities and powers, He made a public spectacle of them, triumphing
over them in it.* At the cross God showcased His power over the enemy by using a means that seemed like utter weakness and defeat.
And in so doing He made a public spectacle of the evil principalities
and powers. In a similar fashion God desires to use His people today
on a continuous basis to display His power to the principalities and
powers in the heavenly places.

Now consider the indicators of the Philistine Curse. The Philistines and the Israelites were continuing adversaries, constantly fighting each other. Come with me to 1 Samuel 13:19-22 to look at a telltale sign of the Philistine Curse.

> *Now there was no blacksmith to be found throughout all the land of Israel, for the Philistines said, "Lest the Hebrews make swords or spears."* [20] *But all the Israelites would go down to the Philistines to sharpen each man's plowshare, his mattock, his ax, and his sickle;* [21] *and the charge for a sharpening was a pim for the plowshares, the mattocks, the forks, and the axes, and to set the points of the goads.* [22] *So it came about, on the day of battle, that there was neither sword nor spear found in the hand of any of the people who were with Saul and Jonathan. But they were found with Saul and Jonathan his son.*

Just as the Israelites lacked the ability to make weapons, so those individuals under the Philistine Curse today lack one essential ingredient or component in order to acquire the rest of what they need to walk out their destiny. You lack that one key item to enable you to advance. If Israel had had blacksmith shops they would have been able to arm themselves, construct better farming tools, and enter into international commerce. When the Philistines took away the blacksmith's shops they stole Israel's chance to succeed.

Another Biblical example of this curse is found in Genesis chapter 26:12-17 where we read,

> *Then Isaac sowed in that land, and reaped in the same year a hundredfold; and the LORD blessed him.* [13] *The man began to prosper, and continued prospering until he became very prosperous;* [14] *for he had possessions of flocks and possessions of herds and a great number of servants. So the Philistines envied him.* [15] *Now the Philistines had stopped up all the wells which his father's servants had dug in the days of Abraham his father, and they had filled them with earth.* [16] *And Abimelech said to*

Isaac, "Go away from us, for you are much mightier than we." [17] *Then Isaac departed from there and pitched his tent in the Valley of Gerar, and dwelt there.*

Because Isaac possessed many cattle he totally depended on an adequate water supply. For the Philistines to stop up the wells meant that they had robbed Isaac of his means of making a living. Many capable and talented Christian people have everything that it takes to be successful. They were voted the most likely to succeed by their graduating class. They appear to be winners and yet, there is something that holds them back and they can't get through certain barriers that less talented individuals easily overcome. They may be highly intelligent and educated, but they lack that one crucial ingredient, which could be a certain certification, a specific skill set, the approval of an executive officer, not knowing the right person, not passing a specific part of a test to gain the right credentialing, etc. If you can't land a job because you lack a required credential and you try and try but can't earn the credential that is an indicator of the Philistine Curse.

Let's say the person applies at his local bank for a necessary loan for a startup company that requires immediate action. The application gets assigned to a loan officer who places it on his desk to deal with after he goes on a much-needed four-day vacation. Towards the end of the get-away he contracts a serious viral infection which puts him out of commission for another two weeks. In the meantime the application gets lost under a mountain of other important papers so the loan officer doesn't get to it until it's too late for the frustrated entrepreneur to make the deal. This scenario aptly describes the Philistine Curse.

An indicator of the Philistine Curse is one that may not have anything to do with the lack of tangible assets but with favor. In this way the Philistine Curse looks something like the Moabite Curse in that the person doesn't receive respect or affirmation in his work. In the Moabite Curse the authority simply does not wish to let the person go where they feel called to go. On the other hand, with the

Philistine Curse the authority actually doesn't grasp the capability of the individual they lead. The person under their authority gets reduced in importance to a significantly lower position than is warranted. The boss truly doesn't see their competency, skill, and dedication. They change jobs trying to get a new start under a different authority but soon discover that the same circumstances occur again.

Another distinguishing mark of the Philistine Curse is the lack of longstanding relationships. Consider Samson, the man that defeated the Philistines. Samson seemed incapable of building meaningful relationships. He didn't destroy the Philistines because of a mighty army he amassed—he did it by himself. He suffered from a dysfunctional marriage and his relationship with his parents was also disjointed. People operating under this curse often experience difficulty in building and sustaining life-giving, nourishing relationships. A healthy individual will go through life accumulating more and more relationships. As I write these words I am serving at a church we joined a little over a year ago. Ruthie and I have built some new friendships where we're at now but I stay in contact with some of the people I pastored many years ago. That accumulative effect is good, and right, and proper but the Philistine Curse seeks to undermine this process of accruing friendships. Let me say it another way, you can't walk out your destiny as a Lone Ranger. God wired us to live and function successfully in community. To live in community is the greatest factor in our success of accomplishing all that God has planned for our lives.

THE SIGNIFICANCY LIE

How does the Philistine Curse gain entry into our bloodline? The significancy lie is that, "I am significant when I obtain power through the truth I know." The trap the person with the motivational gift of teacher often succumbs to is seeking empowerment, importance, significancy through the information they know and can communicate. A variation of this lie in the church is, "I am significant when I know truth revealed to me by God," or "I am significant when I discover hidden nuggets of truth in the Bible."

Sometimes a teacher will seek significancy through the degrees that he holds or the diplomas hanging on the wall. Your true source of significancy lies in what God says about you and if you seek it through the things you know or the degrees you've earned you have sinned. You have embraced a significancy lie. Remember, your significance comes from God alone and what He says about you.

Another way this curse alights is when we or someone in our generational flow place more value in relationships above the truth. In Genesis 21:22-24 we read, *And it came to pass at that time that Abimelech and Phichol, the commander of his army, spoke to Abraham, saying, "God is with you in all that you do.²³ Now therefore, swear to me by God that you will not deal falsely with me, with my offspring, or with my posterity; but that according to the kindness that I have done to you, you will do to me and to the land in which you have dwelt."²⁴ And Abraham said, "I will swear."*

Abraham had been living for decades in the Philistine area and the Philistines had many opportunities to scrutinize him. Think about the total lack of parity between Abraham and the Philistines. Abraham as a bedouin owned no land, had no walled cities, no standing army, no alliances with other countries for protection. The Philistines, on the other hand, had all of these advantages and more. From a human point of view Abraham was defenseless if the Philistines attacked.

With this background in mind, it astonishes me that the Philistine leader, Phichol, approached Abraham proposing they make a covenant agreement with each other. They observed how greatly the favor of the LORD was upon Abraham. Let's put this in perspective. Lesotho is a tiny country in the middle of South Africa with a little less than two million in population. Russia, a military and an economic power with a population of over 143 million, approaches the Lesotho leadership and says, "We see your god at work in your lives and we fear that someday your god will become angry at us and want to destroy us. Please enter into an alliance with us, promising never to harm us." I know, that scenario sounds absurd because Russia obviously would never do such a thing but it was just as strange for the Philistines to make a treaty with Abraham.

Abraham entered into an alliance with Philistia but notice that they acknowledged that the power of Abraham's God was greater than their god Dagon. They received a revelation of the truth regarding the greatness of Yahweh but they declined to commit their lives to Him. If they knew in their hearts that Yahweh possessed greater power than their god why wouldn't they commit to Him? They didn't want to violate family and friend relationships and their cultural customs.

Many individuals today believe the truth revealed in Scripture about various subjects but they fail to adopt those truths and make them their own. They fail to live out the truth, they don't experience the truth. And they decide to not walk out the truth for fear of offending people they're close to. To say it bluntly, they exalt personal relationships above the power of God's truth.

Come with me to the book of I Samuel chapter five where we see the Philistines doing the same thing with the truth. Beginning in verse one we read,

> *Then the Philistines took the ark of God and brought it from Ebenezer to Ashdod.* [2] *When the Philistines took the ark of God, they brought it into the house of Dagon and set it by Dagon.* [3] *And when the people of Ashdod arose early in the morning, there was Dagon, fallen on its face to the earth before the ark of the LORD. So they took Dagon and set it in its place again.* [4] *And when they arose early the next morning, there was Dagon, fallen on its face to the ground before the ark of the LORD. The head of Dagon and both the palms of its hands were broken off on the threshold; only Dagon's torso was left of it.* [5] *Therefore neither the priests of Dagon nor any who come into Dagon's house tread on the threshold of Dagon in Ashdod to this day.*

⁶ But the hand of the LORD was heavy on the people of Ashdod, and He ravaged them and struck them with tumors, both Ashdod and its territory. ⁷ And when the men of Ashdod saw how it was, they said, "The ark of the God of Israel must not remain with us, for His hand is harsh toward us and Dagon our god."⁸ Therefore they sent and gathered to themselves all the lords of the Philistines, and said, "What shall we do with the ark of the God of Israel?"

And they answered, "Let the ark of the God of Israel be carried away to Gath." So they carried the ark of the God of Israel away. ⁹ So it was, after they had carried it away, that the hand of the LORD was against the city with a very great destruction; and He struck the men of the city, both small and great, and tumors broke out on them.

¹⁰ Therefore they sent the ark of God to Ekron. So it was, as the ark of God came to Ekron, that the Ekronites cried out, saying, "They have brought the ark of the God of Israel to us, to kill us and our people!"¹¹ So they sent and gathered together all the lords of the Philistines, and said, "Send away the ark of the God of Israel, and let it go back to its own place, so that it does not kill us and our people." For there was a deadly destruction throughout all the city; the hand of God was very heavy there. ¹² And the men who did not die were stricken with the tumors, and the cry of the city went up to heaven.

They clearly witnessed the power of God first hand. They experienced the reality of Yahweh's greatness over Dagon. Yet they refused to commit themselves to the truth that Yahweh is greater than all other gods. They didn't want to offend their countrymen. In short, they exalted relationships above the truth. The Bible records other instances where the power of God prevailed against the Philistines.

Think of how history would have changed had they embraced the truth that was revealed to them.

So how do we break this curse? We have to be willing to speak the truth in love and live out the truth in a way that shines light on those who don't adopt the truth and who use truth to control. That's what Jesus did. The Scribes and the Pharisees constantly came after Jesus because He spoke the truth and lived out the truth. The way He lived His life served as sort of a silent reprimand to those who refused to embrace the truth. As in the case of Jesus, we too have to be willing to suffer the loss of relationships for the sake of living out the truth.

PRAYER TO BREAK THE PHILISTINE CURSE

"Most High God, I reject, renounce, and break all agreements with the sins that opened the door for the Philistine Curse. I humbly ask You to open the books of my family line and identify every one of my ancestors who operated in the Philistine Curse and please identify every significancy lie they believed. I reject and renounce the lie that says, "I am significant when I obtain power through the truth I know." I ask You, Lord, to identify every circumstance where there was an authority in my family line or in charge of my family line who failed to see the competency in those under their leadership and I confess this behavior as sin. I confess and renounce the sin of my ancestors for failing to construct a launching pad for success for those under their authority and by not recognizing and valuing their gifts, talents, skill sets, and competency.

I also ask You to identify every occurrence where an ancestor chose to value relationships at the expense of speaking and living out the truth. I confess that this is cowardice and that it is sin. I reject, renounce and break all agreements with the fear of man in my life and in the lives of my generations past.

I ask You, Father, to identify every situation where someone in my bloodline looked to the occult to find knowledge and I confess and renounce that as sin. I acknowledge that some of my ancestors used the truth to control others. This is sinful because Your truth is intended to set people free.

Lord, cover these sins related to the Philistine Curse with the blood of Jesus Christ, Your Son. I admit to You Lord, that it was just, right, and proper for this curse to come into my generational line because of sin. I accept Your justice in permitting the devil to consume my generational line because of these bad choices, but I appeal to the finished work of Christ on Calvary's cross, and to His shed blood which is more than powerful enough to break any curse. I send the Philistine Curse in my life and in my bloodline to the cross of Christ, in Jesus' Name. And I declare, in Jesus' Name, that this curse is rendered null and void. I bow my knee and heart to the authority of the Lord Jesus Christ and declare that He is my Lord.

I declare that my spouse, my children, and I are now cleansed of the Philistine Curse, in Jesus' Name. I command that any and every demon sent to empower this curse are now reassigned to dry places. Leave now and never return, in Jesus' Name. I decree and declare that the Philistine Curse in my life is now broken, in Jesus' Name. I ask You Father to release every blessing that has been blocked by the Philistine Curse and restore the years the locusts have eaten. Thank You for those blessings that have been accumulated for us in heaven, in Jesus' Name, Amen."

Chapter Thirteen
THE CANAANITE CURSE

THE FOURTH OF THE CURSES IN THE BOOK OF JUDGES IS THE Canaanite Curse and it corresponds to the fourth motivational gift, the gift of exhortation. The fourth enemy that the Children of Israel faced was the Canaanites. According to the order they come into view in the book of Judges the Canaanites present the fourth of the enemies of Israel. Judges chapter four gives us the historical backdrop surrounding the Canaanite Curse.

> When Ehud was dead, the children of Israel again did evil in the sight of the LORD. ² So the LORD sold them into the hand of Jabin king of Canaan, who reigned in Hazor. The commander of his army was Sisera, who dwelt in Harosheth Hagoyim. ³ And the children of Israel cried out to the LORD; for Jabin had nine hundred chariots of iron, and for twenty years he had harshly oppressed the children of Israel.
>
> ⁴ Now Deborah, a prophetess, the wife of Lapidoth, was judging Israel at that time. ⁵ And she would sit under the palm tree of Deborah between Ramah and Bethel in the mountains of Ephraim. And the children of Israel came up to her for judgment. ⁶ Then she sent and called for Barak the son of Abinoam from Kedesh in Naphtali, and said to him, "Has not the LORD God of Israel commanded, 'Go and deploy troops at Mount Tabor; take with you ten thousand men of the sons of Naphtali and of the sons of Zebulun; ⁷ and against you I will deploy

Sisera, the commander of Jabin's army, with his chariots and his multitude at the River Kishon; and I will deliver him into your hand'?"

8 And Barak said to her, "If you will go with me, then I will go; but if you will not go with me, I will not go!"

9 So she said, "I will surely go with you; nevertheless there will be no glory for you in the journey you are taking, for the LORD will sell Sisera into the hand of a woman." Then Deborah arose and went with Barak to Kedesh. 10 And Barak called Zebulun and Naphtali to Kedesh; he went up with ten thousand men under his command, and Deborah went up with him.

11 Now Heber the Kenite, of the children of Hobab the father-in-law of Moses, had separated himself from the Kenites and pitched his tent near the terebinth tree at Zaanaim, which is beside Kedesh.

12 And they reported to Sisera that Barak the son of Abinoam had gone up to Mount Tabor. 13 So Sisera gathered together all his chariots, nine hundred chariots of iron, and all the people who were with him, from Harosheth Hagoyim to the River Kishon.

14 Then Deborah said to Barak, "Up! For this is the day in which the LORD has delivered Sisera into your hand. Has not the LORD gone out before you?" So Barak went down from Mount Tabor with ten thousand men following him. 15 And the LORD routed Sisera and all his chariots and all his army with the edge of the sword before Barak; and Sisera alighted from his chariot and fled away on foot. 16 But Barak pursued the chariots and the army as far as Harosheth Hagoyim, and all the army of Sisera fell by the edge of the sword; not a man was left.

¹⁷ However, Sisera had fled away on foot to the tent of Jael, the wife of Heber the Kenite; for there was peace between Jabin king of Hazor and the house of Heber the Kenite. ¹⁸ And Jael went out to meet Sisera, and said to him, "Turn aside, my lord, turn aside to me; do not fear." And when he had turned aside with her into the tent, she covered him with a blanket.

¹⁹ Then he said to her, "Please give me a little water to drink, for I am thirsty." So she opened a jug of milk, gave him a drink, and covered him. ²⁰ And he said to her, "Stand at the door of the tent, and if any man comes and inquires of you, and says, 'Is there any man here?' you shall say, 'No.' "

²¹ Then Jael, Heber's wife, took a tent peg and took a hammer in her hand, and went softly to him and drove the peg into his temple, and it went down into the ground; for he was fast asleep and weary. So he died. ²² And then, as Barak pursued Sisera, Jael came out to meet him, and said to him, "Come, I will show you the man whom you seek." And when he went into her tent, there lay Sisera, dead with the peg in his temple.

²³ So on that day God subdued Jabin king of Canaan in the presence of the children of Israel. ²⁴ And the hand of the children of Israel grew stronger and stronger against Jabin king of Canaan, until they had destroyed Jabin king of Canaan.

Deborah was the first female leader in the nation of Israel. Many years beforehand, Miriam, Moses' sister, filled a leadership role of sorts in that she had a level of influence but she did not lead in an official capacity as did Deborah. God had raised her up as a judge and the Israelite men came to her to settle their disputes and obtain guidance in legal arbitration. In that culture women typically did not rise to recognized, official leadership positions but God had raised her up and men followed her.

It seems that God gave Deborah a prophetic word for General Barak. God said, "Go this day and take ten thousand soldiers with you and I will deliver Sisera, the commander of Jabin's army, into your hands." God had it all set up for Barak's victory. God promised He would deliver the enemy into Barak's hands. Yet, even though he had ten thousand soldiers, and even though he had a promise of victory from God, he told Deborah, "I won't go unless you come with me." Go figure. Why would he say that? I believe it is because he lacked a true sense of significancy.

THE SIGNIFICANCY LIE

As previously stated, the Canaanite Curse corresponds to the gift of exhortation, the fourth of the motivational gifts. The exhorter often falls into the significancy lie that says, "I am significant when people want and need to be around me." The non-secular version of this lie is, "I am significant when a lot of people need my spiritual resources to walk in their God-ordained destiny." While the prophet likes to fix problems, and the servant likes to build a launching pad for success under other people, and the teacher likes to gain knowledge, the exhorter needs to have people gathered around him that want and need to be in his company. Through the significancy lie of the exhorters they often become some of the most abusive leaders who prey on the people under their authority and in the church they cause much trauma through spiritual abuse.

One of the indicators that someone is under the Canaanite Curse is that they are apt to go from one abusive leader to another. Those in authority will frequently exploit them in some fashion. Some people go to a spiritually abusive church and get wounded and leave. They find another church that seems much better but soon they discover that the leadership is just as exploitive as the last church and this pattern happens time and time again. Individuals under the Canaanite Curse are drawn to abusive church leadership or to abusive, predatory bosses in the secular environment.

When the Canaanite Curse is active in an individual that person is apt to join a church or find employment with a business where the authority, the pastor or boss, claims to see great things in store for him. The pastor or boss will underscore the ability and talent and the value he adds to the organization. And in a relatively short time he will advance to a significant position, but all these promises never come to fruition. The truth is, the leader will say anything to reel the person in so that he can use the individual to support the organization rather than helping the person succeed.

Another way the effects of this curse get played out is that the abilities and talents of the individual are made light of or minimized. Often the Moabite Curse and the Canaanite Curse team up together making it very difficult for the person to walk in his God-given destiny and do what God has called him to do. He finds himself in continuous training to be competent enough but in the leader's mind that day never comes. He never gets released into his calling because the leader needs the person to rely on him for his wisdom, knowledge, expertise, and anointing. The healthy role of the leader, whether it be the parents, the ministry leader, or the pastor is to equip them and release them. Sadly the Canaanite leader has a hard time releasing those he equipped because he needs people to need him and that's how this leader gets his significancy.

Now let's take a look at how the Canaanite Curse originated. In Genesis 9:20-27 we read,

> *And Noah began to be a farmer, and he planted a vineyard. [21] Then he drank of the wine and was drunk, and became uncovered in his tent. [22] And Ham, the father of Canaan, saw the nakedness of his father, and told his two brothers outside. [23] But Shem and Japheth took a garment, laid it on both their shoulders, and went backward and covered the nakedness of their father. Their fac-*

es were turned away, and they did not see their father's nakedness.

[24] So Noah awoke from his wine, and knew what his younger son had done to him. [25] Then he said: "Cursed be Canaan; a servant of servants he shall be to his brethren." [26] And he said: "Blessed be the LORD, the God of Shem, and may Canaan be his servant. [27] May God enlarge Japheth, and may he dwell in the tents of Shem; and may Canaan be his servant."

God severely cursed Canaan by making him a slave to his brothers. His father, Ham, actually committed the sin but Canaan got cursed. Perhaps this illustrates how the iniquity of the father gets passed on to their children. What Ham did was similar to viewing pornography but worse because he dishonored his father. It doesn't say he touched his father, he only looked. Ham not only sinned by his inappropriate looking, he tried to make it okay by getting his brothers to participate in the evil deed. When "everybody's doing it" it makes us feel all right about our sin.

Canaan's father brought this curse through his efforts to make his sin normal. Then Canaan, as a nation, predatorily oppressed the Children of Israel. In the end the Canaanites were annihilated and are not in existence today. In the same way authorities under the Canaanite Curse, who tend to repeatedly exploit those under them, open the way for the enemy to eventually devastate them.

Leaders who empower this curse are those, like Ham, who use their influence to normalize evil. People who walk free of this curse learn to be like Deborah. They accept that they are significant because of God's appointment, because of what God says about them. They don't need the approval of others, they don't need followers, they know God has called them to a certain job despite the criticism of the naysayers around them. They are willing to stand alone against popular sin in religious and secular environments. They are willing to be the only voice speaking out proclaiming the way to resolve the troublesome, perplexing issues.

God wants Christian leaders who are so at peace in the pursuit of their God-ordained mission, their significance, their validity that they are willing to speak out against a sinful action or attitude in the church even though most of the believers are involved in it. God wants leaders to be like Barak, who was under Deborah's authority, who will lead their followers into risky battles God gives them to fight. Deborah put her reputation on the line by leading those under her authority into a battle they could have easily lost and God honors that depth of faith. Her degree of faith destroys the Canaanite Curse.

When the Canaanite Curse is broken individuals are empowered to expand the resources that God has given them. God's people owned the fertile Jordan Valley but because the Canaanites controlled that area it was worthless to Israel. Israel owned it but they couldn't use it for crops or livestock or anything else until the Canaanites were forced to leave. For Israel victory came in stages. First, Sisera was killed, then God subdued Jabin, and thirdly, Israel gradually grew stronger and stronger until, lastly, they destroyed Jabin. Sometimes we go through a slow but sure process of breaking the Canaanite Curse.

PRAYER TO BREAK THE CANAANITE CURSE

"Abba Father, I confess and renounce my sin and the sin of my ancestors for seeking to normalize our sin by getting others to participate in it. Heavenly Father, I ask You to open the books of my life and in the lives of our ancestors to locate any time one of us looked to popularity as our source of significancy. I reject, renounce, and break all agreements with the lie that significancy can be obtained through popularity. I know that sometimes some of my ancestors believed that lie and I confess that as sin. I reject and renounce the spirit of denial that declines to be aware of the rebukes of life. I confess and renounce the sin of shifting the consequences of one's poor decisions to those under their authority. I confess and renounce in my family line the sin of leaders exploiting and wrongfully using those under their authority. I reject and renounce the twisted approach of appealing to love, loyalty or submission in order to compel those under us to pay the price for our poor choices and sins. I reject, renounce and break all agreements with the deception of conducting oneself in love, loyalty and submission to pay the price for their leader's sin. I reject and renounce the entitlement spirit and I declare that whatsoever a man sows, that shall he also reap, that Godly sowing is required in order to reap a Godly harvest. I reject and renounce the implementation of visions that necessitate the exploitation of God's children and I reject and renounce validating those visions in God's name. I reject and renounce using popularity to regularize injustice and imbalance. I reject and renounce my sin and the sin of my ancestors in lowering God's holy standards. I confess the sin of remaining in an abusive position to the extent that we could not walk out our calling. I confess the sin of remaining in a situation in which we were not supposed to be just so that we could keep the peace and not upset the apple cart. I ask You Lord to cleanse my family line of the iniquity of the Canaanite Curse and I receive this cleansing in the mighty Name of Jesus Christ. I command every demonic spirit that was sent to enforce and empower the Canaanite Curse to leave me now and never return, in the Name of Jesus. I decree and declare, in Jesus' Name, that the Canaanite Curse is broken. It no longer affects my life. I ask you to extend this cleansing to my spouse, children and to my children's children. I ask You Father to give me Your plan and Your timing and Your techniques to completely demolish the Canaanite Curse and its effects upon my life. Lord show me if I need to leave an organization or ministry so that I can mature in my gifting and fulfill Your plan for my life. And Lord I ask You to not only show me how but to supernaturally empower me to walk out my destiny, in the Name of Jesus Christ, Amen."

Chapter Fourteen
THE MIDIANITE CURSE

THE FIFTH OF THE SEVEN CURSES IN THE BOOK OF JUDGES IS THE Midianite Curse and this curse corresponds to the fifth motivational gift, the gift of giving. As this story opens, Gideon, is down in a wine press threshing wheat. Everybody knows that you don't thresh wheat down in a wine press, you go up on the top of a hill where there's plenty of wind to blow away the chaff as the wheat is tossed into the air. Why was he down in a wine press? Because of the Midianite threat. He was hiding due to the fact that the Midianites came in hoards every Spring and devoured their harvest.

Let's begin by looking at the ravaging effects the Midianite Curse had upon the Children of Israel as told in Judges 6:1-13.

> *Then the children of Israel did evil in the sight of the LORD. So the LORD delivered them into the hand of Midian for seven years, ² and the hand of Midian prevailed against Israel. Because of the Midianites, the children of Israel made for themselves the dens, the caves, and the strongholds which are in the mountains. ³ So it was, whenever Israel had sown, Midianites would come up; also Amalekites and the people of the East would come up against them. ⁴ Then they would encamp against them and destroy the produce of the earth as far as Gaza, and leave no sustenance for Israel, neither sheep nor ox nor donkey. ⁵ For they would come up with their livestock and their tents, coming in as numerous as locusts; both they and their camels were without number; and they would enter the land to destroy it. ⁶ So Israel*

was greatly impoverished because of the Midianites, and the children of Israel cried out to the LORD.

[7] And it came to pass, when the children of Israel cried out to the LORD because of the Midianites,[8] that the LORD sent a prophet to the children of Israel, who said to them, "Thus says the LORD God of Israel: 'I brought you up from Egypt and brought you out of the house of bondage;[9] and I delivered you out of the hand of the Egyptians and out of the hand of all who oppressed you, and drove them out before you and gave you their land.[10] Also I said to you, "I am the LORD your God; do not fear the gods of the Amorites, in whose land you dwell." But you have not obeyed My voice.'"

[11] Now the Angel of the LORD came and sat under the terebinth tree which was in Ophrah, which belonged to Joash the Abiezrite, while his son Gideon threshed wheat in the winepress, in order to hide it from the Midianites.[12] And the Angel of the LORD appeared to him, and said to him, "The LORD is with you, you mighty man of valor!"

[13] Gideon said to Him, "O my lord, if the LORD is with us, why then has all this happened to us? And where are all His miracles which our fathers told us about, saying, 'Did not the LORD bring us up from Egypt?' But now the LORD has forsaken us and delivered us into the hands of the Midianites."

Like Israel in Gideon's day, people who operate under the Midianite Curse often experience seasonal ravaging. For example, a husband and wife work hard all year to save up a little nest egg, enough for a decent down payment on a new home. They diligently stay within the bounds of their budget, accept any overtime their employers offer, and are careful to avoid any frivolous expenditures. They faithfully tithe to their local church and give to worthwhile causes. Things look very good until the end of April when the bottom falls out. The refrigerator stops running and has to be replaced, both cars break down and need major repairs, the hot water heater rusts out and floods the home, and the kids need major emergency dental work until, almost overnight, all of their savings vanish. To the dismay of this married couple, this scenario is not a one-time problem, they suffer from a similar frustrating ravaging about the same time every year making it impossible to get ahead.

The inability to get ahead often follows those who are under the Midianite Curse. They start a business and as soon as it begins to take off, as soon as it begins to operate in the black, something happens and the business crashes. Some people work and work to pay off a major debt and about the time it gets paid off an emergency arises and they're back in debt.

Most commonly for those under the Midianite Curse the ravaging seems to be seasonal but the pattern of financial devastation may happen in different ways. For example, one woman experienced the ravaging every odd number of years. I asked another person I ministered to, to think about any time patterns related to past traumatic events. After giving it some careful thought she realized that devastations occurred at various times in the calendar year but it always happened on the 16th of the month. While in a ministry session with another person and listening to her story we discovered that for her the devastation happened every seven years. I ministered to a man who experienced a ten-year pattern of ravaging. Every tenth year some people suffer through an entire year of devastation.

For those who operate under the Midianite Curse they quite often experience some type of upheaval during the holidays. To illustrate, a man gets sick every December and misses a lot of work making him go without several much-needed paychecks. Things around the house tend to go haywire as it did one Christmas week when the sewer line under the slab floor cracked due to rust or ground settlement, making it impossible to use the plumbing until the sewer got repaired. The plumber had to jackhammer a huge hole in the concrete floor in the middle of the house and dig a tunnel to enable him to get to the damaged pipe. Dirt and concrete dust went everywhere throughout the house even though the plumber did his best to keep the dirt and dust localized. The plumber postponed his work for two days to celebrate Christmas while this poor family suffered continued mishaps.

The cat broke its foot and the vet insisted it have surgery. The wife backed up into the neighbor's new Infinity causing over $2,000.00 in damages. His younger brother, who lived several thousand miles away, died in an industrial accident but he was too sick and too broke to make the trip for the funeral. Major mold was discovered in the heating ducts and the dishwasher quit working so the man and his wife can't wait for the month of December to be over and their lives can get back to normal. But the same type of bizarre series of catastrophes happen the following Christmas season. With these kind of seasonal catastrophes it becomes easy for the individuals involved to doubt the goodness of God. Doubting God's goodness compounds the problem because it becomes harder to trust a God who is not good.

With this information in mind let us now go to the well-known story of God using Gideon to deliver the Israelites from the Midianites in Judges chapter seven. Gideon started with 32,000 troops but God said that was too many so the army was whittled down to 10,000. God said that was too many and the number got reduced to 300. Let's pick up beginning with verse 16.

Then he divided the three hundred men into three companies, and he put a trumpet into every man's hand, with empty pitchers, and torches inside the pitchers. [17] And he said to them, "Look at me and do likewise; watch, and when I come to the edge of the camp you shall do as I do. [18] When I blow the trumpet, I and all who are with me, then you also blow the trumpets on every side of the whole camp, and say, 'The sword of the LORD and of Gideon!' "

[19] *So Gideon and the hundred men who were with him came to the outpost of the camp at the beginning of the middle watch, just as they had posted the watch; and they blew the trumpets and broke the pitchers that were in their hands. [20] Then the three companies blew the trumpets and broke the pitchers—they held the torches in their left hands and the trumpets in their right hands for blowing—and they cried, "The sword of the LORD and of Gideon!" [21] And every man stood in his place all around the camp; and the whole army ran and cried out and fled. [22] When the three hundred blew the trumpets, the LORD set every man's sword against his companion throughout the whole camp; and the army fled to Beth Acacia, toward Zererah, as far as the border of Abel Meholah, by Tabbath. [23] And the men of Israel gathered together from Naphtali, Asher, and all Manasseh, and pursued the Midianites.*

[24] Then Gideon sent messengers throughout all the mountains of Ephraim, saying, "Come down against the Midianites, and seize from them the watering places as far as Beth Barah and the Jordan." Then all the men of Ephraim gathered together and seized the watering places as far as Beth Barah and the Jordan. [25] And they captured two princes of the Midianites, Oreb and Zeeb. They killed Oreb at the rock of Oreb, and Zeeb they killed at the winepress of Zeeb. They pursued Midian and brought the heads of Oreb and Zeeb to Gideon on the other side of the Jordan.

Now skip down to chapter eight, verse four.

When Gideon came to the Jordan, he and the three hundred men who were with him crossed over, exhausted but still in pursuit. [5] Then he said to the men of Succoth, "Please give loaves of bread to the people who follow me, for they are exhausted, and I am pursuing

Zebah and Zalmunna, kings of Midian." ⁶ And the leaders of Succoth said, "Are the hands of Zebah and Zalmunna now in your hand, that we should give bread to your army?"

⁷ So Gideon said, "For this cause, when the LORD has delivered Zebah and Zalmunna into my hand, then I will tear your flesh with the thorns of the wilderness and with briers!" ⁸ Then he went up from there to Penuel and spoke to them in the same way. And the men of Penuel answered him as the men of Succoth had answered. ⁹ So he also spoke to the men of Penuel, saying, "When I come back in peace, I will tear down this tower!"

¹⁰ Now Zebah and Zalmunna were at Karkor, and their armies with them, about fifteen thousand, all who were left of all the army of the people of the East; for one hundred and twenty thousand men who drew the sword had fallen. ¹¹ Then Gideon went up by the road of those who dwell in tents on the east of Nobah and Jogbehah; and he attacked the army while the camp felt secure. ¹² When Zebah and Zalmunna fled, he pursued them; and he took the two kings of Midian, Zebah and Zalmunna, and routed the whole army.

¹³ Then Gideon the son of Joash returned from battle, from the Ascent of Heres. ¹⁴ And he caught a young man of the men of Succoth and interrogated him; and he wrote down for him the leaders of Succoth and its elders, seventy-seven men. ¹⁵ Then he came to the men of Succoth and said, "Here are Zebah and Zalmunna, about whom you ridiculed me, saying, 'Are the hands of Zebah and Zalmunna now in your hand, that we should give bread to your weary men?' " ¹⁶ And he took the elders of the city, and thorns of the wilderness and briers, and with them he taught the men of Succoth. ¹⁷ Then he tore down the tower of Penuel and killed the men of the city.

[18] And he said to Zebah and Zalmunna, "What kind of men were they whom you killed at Tabor?" So they answered, "As you are, so were they; each one resembled the son of a king."

[19] Then he said, "They were my brothers, the sons of my mother. As the LORD lives, if you had let them live, I would not kill you."[20] And he said to Jether his firstborn, "Rise, kill them!" But the youth would not draw his sword; for he was afraid, because he was still a youth.

[21] So Zebah and Zalmunna said, "Rise yourself, and kill us; for as a man is, so is his strength." So Gideon arose and killed Zebah and Zalmunna, and took the crescent ornaments that were on their camels' necks.[22] Then the men of Israel said to Gideon, "Rule over us, both you and your son, and your grandson also; for you have delivered us from the hand of Midian."[23] But Gideon said to them, "I will not rule over you, nor shall my son rule over you; the LORD shall rule over you."

As we study the names of the people involved in this story we can gain some insights about the Midianite Curse. One prince's name is Oreb and Oreb means "raven." If you've ever watched ravens they are not very particular about what they eat. After all, they will eat decaying road kill. That's the way this curse functions. It is very creative in the way it eats up our resources. For instance, you think you have enough homeowner's insurance but it will find a way to devour something the insurance policy does not cover, or you think you have great medical coverage but it will find something the medical plan excludes.

The name Zeeb means "wolf." Wolves like to stalk a herd of animals and focus on the weak and the elderly that lag behind the rest of the herd. The hardest negative effect of the Midianite Curse is the damage it does to personal relationships as a result of the financial devastation. Financial devastation does not automatically lead to damaged lives. The key is in how we respond to financial struggles.

A colleague of mine, another prayer minister, ministered to a woman, who in the process of telling her story, told of how as a small child her mother and siblings went dumpster diving to find their daily food. My colleague said that when she heard this part of the story she was aghast and expected to hear a response that reflected deep trauma. She asked the counselee, "How did it feel to have to get your dinner out of a dumpster?" The lady replied, "Oh, we loved it! Mom made it a game—it was great fun." It was not a traumatic memory. Trauma, deep wounding, often comes, not because of the bad things that happen to us, but it comes from the way we respond to the bad things that happen.

Financial devastation is not the problem. In the midst of financial destruction, the real problem comes when Zeeb, the wolf, is success-ful in destroying relationships, to cause division, and marital stress. We are told that the number one cause of divorce seems to be finan-cial problems but that is, in part, because Zeeb uses financial lack to drive a wedge between loved ones and friends.

It is important also to look at the names of the two kings, Zebah and Zalmunna. The name Zebah speaks of the lack of defense from being sacrificed. Families that own a flock of sheep would often des-ignate some to be sacrificed but there might be one or two that were loved and thought of as pets. Pets would not be sacrificed, they were protected. However, the rest of the sheep lacked that protection and could be selected for a sacrifice.

The name Zalmunna speaks of lacking the protection of shade. In that desert region shade was a necessity. And we expect certain sys-tems and institutions in our life to protect us from the vicissitudes of everyday life and one of those is family. Family relationships should serve as a source of protection and solace from the trials of life. Those under the Midianite Curse may feel as though the normal protections that family relationships provide to help us recover and get revitalized are not in place and it becomes very difficult to relax and unwind. This is one of the indicators of the Midianite Curse.

THE SIGNIFICANCY LIE

As stated, the Midianite Curse, the fifth of the curses in the book of Judges, corresponds to the fifth motivational gift listed in Romans 12, the gift of giving. Some people are especially gifted and motivated to give money, or food, or time, or skill. However, the significancy lie is, "I am significant when I can supply the wherewithal for others to walk in their God-ordained destiny." That is the task God has given them but that is not a legitimate source of significance. The giver's calling is the same as the prophet's in the sense that they are supposed to fix things, but their significance does not come from fulfilling their calling, it comes from God Himself.

The pitfall for the giver is that they fail to understand the difference between giving and investing. All Christians are called to tithe and give up and beyond the tithe but the giver has the ability to give more wisely than the other six gifts. The giver knows how to give strategically in a way that will empower another person to be successful in their calling. So the giver's temptation is to control, to give with strings attached. In their minds they want to insure that the resources go to the right place but very often their motives are wrong - they want to control. Sometimes the giver has a need to be needed and consequently others can develop an unwholesome dependence on him. They sometimes believe the significancy lie that says, "I am significant when others need me," or "I am significant when others are dependent on me at all times." Therefore, it becomes very important that the giver receives heart revelation knowledge that one's significancy comes from what God says, not from giving. Also the giver must give out of obedience to God's direction, not for the sake of being needed or the desire to control.

Now let's look at the origin of the Midianite nation. In Genesis 25: 1-5 we read,

> *Abraham again took a wife, and her name was Keturah. ² And she bore him Zimran, Jokshan, Medan, Midian, Ishbak, and Shuah. ³ Jokshan begot Sheba and Dedan. And the sons of Dedan were Asshurim, Letushim, and Le-*

ummim. ⁴ And the sons of Midian were Ephah, Epher, Hanoch, Abidah, and Eldaah. All these were the children of Keturah. ⁵ And Abraham gave all that he had to Isaac. ⁶ But Abraham gave gifts to the sons of the concubines which Abraham had; and while he was still living he sent them eastward, away from Isaac his son, to the country of the east.

This passage of Scripture talks about what happened to Abraham after the death of his wife, Sarah. Abraham's original name was Abram, meaning "exalted father" or "high father." When he was 99 years old God changed his name to Abraham, meaning "father of a multitude" or "father of many." God's plan for Abraham was that his descendants would bless all nations, but how could that happen if he had no biological son? After waiting many years for his wife Sarah to get pregnant he took matters into his own hands by taking Hagar to be his concubine, who gave birth to Ishmael and great conflict arose between the Ishmaelites and the Israelites and continues to this day. After the birth of Ishmael Abraham waited another 13 long years before Sarah gave birth to the promised seed, Isaac.

This was Abraham's God-ordained destiny, to give birth to the promised son whose descendants would bless the earth. Once Isaac was born it was Abraham's job to protect, guide, mentor, and serve as a positive role model to his son. After Sarah's death, however, Abraham once again lost sight of his calling. Apparently he sought after comfort by hitching up to another concubine. He put comfort ahead of his calling. He took Keturah as his concubine. He didn't even have the guts to enter into a covenant relationship with her through full marriage. Concubines did not have the same status as wives. Through this "affair" with Keturah he became the biological father of six more sons, one of whom was Midian. Eventually he sent Keturah away along with her six sons. He sent them to the east because he came to see the potential problem they caused for his son Isaac. Isaac was his main responsibility, but perhaps because of his loneliness, the heartache of losing his beloved wife, he took Keturah into his life. Instead of investing his remaining years into Isaac, preparing, influencing, equipping, and empowering him, he got sidetracked because he thought he needed the comfort of a live-in female companion. And because of his selfish desire, because he wasn't walking in his God-ordained destiny, Midian became the perennial enemy of the descendants of Isaac, the Jewish nation. And people who put comfort ahead of their calling open the door for the Midianite Curse.

Breaking this curse involves more than just reciting a prayer. The person under this curse must sincerely desire to walk in their God-given destiny to the extent that they are willing to forego comfort and security if necessary. They must be willing to risk whatever it takes to walk out God's call upon their life and become totally dependent on God. If their motivational gift is giving they must be willing to give as God directs without any need to be needed and without a desire to control.

When the Midianite Curse is broken what can you expect? First, the seasonal ravaging will cease, but there's a greater blessing than that. For instance, if the Christmas holiday has been cursed, that time of year will become a tremendous blessing as God pours out His abundant supply and reveals His majestic power and glory. Certain times of the year that Satan has used in the past will become seasons used for the glory of God. But we have to be proactive in fervent prayer and expectancy that God will redeem those periods of time knowing that what the enemy used for evil, God intends to use for good.

PRAYER TO BREAK THE MIDIANITE CURSE

"Heavenly Father, I declare that You are the God of time. Time is the first thing You created on the first day, therefore, time is the first fruits of Your creation. And the first fruits of everything are dedicated to You and in this way time is made Holy. So I declare that since I am Your child, Your intent for me was to walk in a Holy time. It is not Your plan for the seasons of my life to bring devastation. I acknowledge that the ravaging, the devastation related to time is the result of sin, in my life and/or in the lives of my generations past, that someone in my generational flow who had the gift of giving, used their gift to control. I confess this behavior as sin and I renounce it. Lord, I ask You to open the books of my family line and identify every time one of my ancestors used their gift to control. I renounce, reject, and break all agreements with the spirit of control in my life and in every branch of my family line. I confess, reject and renounce the significancy lie that says, "I am significant when I provide the resources for others to walk in their God-ordained destiny." I reject, renounce, and break all agreements with the spirit of faithlessness that kept some of my ancestors from walking in their God-ordained destiny. I confess, reject and renounce the lie of the enemy that it is right to suspend the pursuit of our destiny until a suitable time. I ask You Father to cleanse my generational bloodline of that iniquity. I confess and renounce the sin of doubting Your goodness. By Your grace the issue of Your goodness is settled in my heart and mind and I declare that God is good. Remove the Midianite Curse from my life, my children, and grandchildren's lives and nail that curse to the cross of Christ. In Jesus' Name, I command that curse to be halted at the cross of Christ along with its effects upon me and my family. Heavenly Father, I decree and declare that I am utterly dependent on You. I confess my sin and the sins of my generations past for seeking comfort above our calling. Please bring that fleshly tendency to death at the cross of Christ. Lord, please give me the faith to walk in the plan You have for my life no matter what the risks. Lord, I believe, but help my unbelief. Every place that the devil used to curse, where Your plan is to loose great blessings, I declare the will of God be done. I ask that the blessings You purposed for me would be released in the seasons You have ordained. I ask You to sanctify and bless the seasons of my life that have been cursed by the enemy, in Jesus' Mighty Name, Amen."

Chapter Fifteen

JOTHAM'S CURSE

THE SIXTH SIGNIFICANCY CURSE IS CALLED JOTHAM'S CURSE AND it corresponds to the sixth motivational gift of ruler, or what is commonly translated as "leader." Take a look at one of the most overlooked stories in the Bible as found in Judges chapter nine.

Then Abimelech the son of Jerubbaal went to Shechem, to his mother's brothers, and spoke with them and with all the family of the house of his mother's father, saying, [2] *"Please speak in the hearing of all the men of Shechem: 'Which is better for you, that all seventy of the sons of Jerubbaal reign over you, or that one reign over you?' Remember that I am your own flesh and bone."*

[3] *And his mother's brothers spoke all these words concerning him in the hearing of all the men of Shechem; and their heart was inclined to follow Abimelech, for they said, "He is our brother."* [4] *So they gave him seventy shekels of silver from the temple of Baal-Berith, with which Abimelech hired worthless and reckless men; and they followed him.* [5] *Then he went to his father's house at Ophrah and killed his brothers, the seventy sons of Jerubbaal, on one stone. But Jotham the youngest son of Jerubbaal was left, because he hid himself.* [6] *And all the men of Shechem gathered together, all of Beth Millo, and they went and made Abimelech king beside the terebinth tree at the pillar that was in Shechem.*

⁷ Now when they told Jotham, he went and stood on top of Mount Gerizim, and lifted his voice and cried out. And he said to them:

> *"Listen to me, you men of Shechem,*
> *That God may listen to you!*

⁸ "The trees once went forth to anoint a king over them.
And they said to the olive tree,
'Reign over us!'

⁹ But the olive tree said to them,
'Should I cease giving my oil,
With which they honor God and men,
And go to sway over trees?'

¹⁰ "Then the trees said to the fig tree,
'You come and reign over us!'

¹¹ But the fig tree said to them,
'Should I cease my sweetness and my good fruit,
And go to sway over trees?'

¹² "Then the trees said to the vine,
'You come and reign over us!'

¹³ But the vine said to them,
'Should I cease my new wine,
Which cheers both God and men,
And go to sway over trees?'

¹⁴ "Then all the trees said to the bramble,
'You come and reign over us!'

¹⁵ And the bramble said to the trees,
'If in truth you anoint me as king over you,
Then come and take shelter in my shade;
But if not, let fire come out of the bramble
And devour the cedars of Lebanon!'

¹⁶ *"Now therefore, if you have acted in truth and sinceri-*
ty in making Abimelech king, and if you have dealt well
with Jerubbaal and his house, and have done to him as
*he deserves —*¹⁷ *for my father fought for you, risked his*
life, and delivered you out of the hand of Midian; ¹⁸ *but*
you have risen up against my father's house this day, and
killed his seventy sons on one stone, and made
Abimelech, the son of his female servant, king over the
*men of Shechem, because he is your brother —*¹⁹ *if then*
you have acted in truth and sincerity with Jerubbaal and
with his house this day, then rejoice in Abimelech, and
let him also rejoice in you. ²⁰ *"But if not, let fire come*
from Abimelech and devour the men of Shechem and
Beth Millo; and let fire come from the men of Shechem
*and from Beth Millo and devour Abimelech!"*²¹ *And*
Jotham ran away and fled; and he went to Beer and
dwelt there, for fear of Abimelech his brother.

²² *After Abimelech had reigned over Israel three*
years, ²³ *God sent a spirit of ill will between Abimelech*
and the men of Shechem; and the men of Shechem dealt
treacherously with Abimelech, ²⁴ *that the crime done to*
the seventy sons of Jerubbaal might be settled and their
blood be laid on Abimelech their brother, who killed
them, and on the men of Shechem, who aided him in
the killing of his brothers. ²⁵ *And the men of Shechem set*
men in ambush against him on the tops of the mountains,
and they robbed all who passed by them along that way;
and it was told Abimelech.

²⁶ *Now Gaal the son of Ebed came with his brothers and*
went over to Shechem; and the men of Shechem put
their confidence in him. ²⁷ *So they went out into the*
fields, and gathered grapes from their vineyards and
trod them, and made merry. And they went into the
house of their god, and ate and drank, and cursed

Abimelech. ²⁸ *Then Gaal the son of Ebed said, "Who is Abimelech, and who is Shechem, that we should serve him? Is he not the son of Jerubbaal, and is not Zebul his officer? Serve the men of Hamor the father of Shechem; but why should we serve him?* ²⁹ *If only this people were under my authority! Then I would remove Abimelech." So he said to Abimelech, "Increase your army and come out!"*

³⁰ *When Zebul, the ruler of the city, heard the words of Gaal the son of Ebed, his anger was aroused.* ³¹ *And he sent messengers to Abimelech secretly, saying, "Take note! Gaal the son of Ebed and his brothers have come to Shechem; and here they are, fortifying the city against you.* ³² *Now therefore, get up by night, you and the people who are with you, and lie in wait in the field.* ³³ *And it shall be, as soon as the sun is up in the morning, that you shall rise early and rush upon the city; and when he and the people who are with him come out against you, you may then do to them as you find opportunity."*

³⁴ *So Abimelech and all the people who were with him rose by night, and lay in wait against Shechem in four companies.* ³⁵ *When Gaal the son of Ebed went out and stood in the entrance to the city gate, Abimelech and the people who were with him rose from lying in wait.* ³⁶ *And when Gaal saw the people, he said to Zebul, "Look, people are coming down from the tops of the mountains!"*

But Zebul said to him, "You see the shadows of the mountains as if they were men."

³⁷ *So Gaal spoke again and said, "See, people are coming down from the center of the land, and another company is coming from the Diviners' Terebinth Tree."*

³⁸ Then Zebul said to him, "Where indeed is your mouth now, with which you said, 'Who is Abimelech, that we should serve him?' Are not these the people whom you despised? Go out, if you will, and fight with them now."

³⁹ So Gaal went out, leading the men of Shechem, and fought with Abimelech.⁴⁰ And Abimelech chased him, and he fled from him; and many fell wounded, to the very entrance of the gate. ⁴¹ Then Abimelech dwelt at Arumah, and Zebul drove out Gaal and his brothers, so that they would not dwell in Shechem.

⁴² And it came about on the next day that the people went out into the field, and they told Abimelech. ⁴³ So he took his people, divided them into three companies, and lay in wait in the field. And he looked, and there were the people, coming out of the city; and he rose against them and attacked them.⁴⁴ Then Abimelech and the company that was with him rushed forward and stood at the entrance of the gate of the city; and the other two companies rushed upon all who were in the fields and killed them. ⁴⁵ So Abimelech fought against the city all that day; he took the city and killed the people who were in it; and he demolished the city and sowed it with salt.

⁴⁶ Now when all the men of the tower of Shechem had heard that, they entered the stronghold of the temple of the god Berith. ⁴⁷ And it was told Abimelech that all the men of the tower of Shechem were gathered together. ⁴⁸ Then Abimelech went up to Mount Zalmon, he and all the people who were with him. And Abimelech took an ax in his hand and cut down a bough from the trees, and took it and laid it on his shoulder; then he said to the people who were with him, "What you have seen me do, make haste and do as I have done."⁴⁹ So each of the people likewise cut down his own bough and fol-

lowed Abimelech, put them against the stronghold, and set the stronghold on fire above them, so that all the people of the tower of Shechem died, about a thousand men and women.

⁵⁰ Then Abimelech went to Thebez, and he encamped against Thebez and took it. ⁵¹ But there was a strong tower in the city, and all the men and women—all the people of the city—fled there and shut themselves in; then they went up to the top of the tower. ⁵² So Abimelech came as far as the tower and fought against it; and he drew near the door of the tower to burn it with fire. ⁵³ But a certain woman dropped an upper millstone on Abimelech's head and crushed his skull. ⁵⁴ Then he called quickly to the young man, his armor bearer, and said to him, "Draw your sword and kill me, lest men say of me, 'A woman killed him.' " So his young man thrust him through, and he died. ⁵⁵ And when the men of Israel saw that Abimelech was dead, they departed, every man to his place.

⁵⁶ Thus God repaid the wickedness of Abimelech, which he had done to his father by killing his seventy brothers. ⁵⁷ And all the evil of the men of Shechem God returned on their own heads, **and on them came the curse of Jotham the son of Jerubbaal** (emphasis added).

The Curse of Jotham represents the hardest of the seven curses to demolish because it didn't involve a judge as did the other significancy curses. In this story people killed each other until there was no one left to fight. The indicator that there exists the Curse of Jotham is the lack of unity. Churches under this curse experience continuous splits over the years. Normally the split is spearheaded by one of the key leaders such as an elder or an associate pastor, an individual who is a trusted friend of the lead pastor. The curse can manifest in parachurch organizations or ministry teams within a church. Division in a ministry team comes like clockwork every nine to ten months and individuals leave the church having been deeply wounded.

A similar dynamic manifests in business partnerships and people under this curse may go from one business partnership to another experiencing betrayal, disloyalty, and frustration. Another common problem for businesses under this curse is that they repeatedly experience a trusted key employee leaving and taking important information or the ex-employee wooing customers away from the company, which actions drain the businesses' capital and prohibit them from moving forward.

Families under the Curse of Jotham continually witness division and strife and this division often occurs generationally. Every generation in the family line suffers a continual pattern of relatives being at odds with other relatives—brother against brother, sister against sister, and cousin against cousin. The pattern of a lack of unity points to the presence of the Curse of Jotham.

The defining moment in the story of Jotham and Abimelek occurred three years into the reign of Abimelek. In verses 23-24 of our focal Scripture passage we read, *God sent a spirit of ill will between Abimelech and the men of Shechem; and the men of Shechem dealt treacherously with Abimelech,* [24] *that the crime done to the seventy sons of Jerubbaal might be settled and their blood be laid on Abimelech their brother, who killed them, and on the men of Shechem, who aided him in the killing of his brothers.*

Just prior to these two verses we find Jotham appealing to the men of Shechem, [19] *if then you have acted in truth and sincerity with Jerubbaal and with his house this day, rejoice in Abimelech, and let him also rejoice in you.* [20] *"But if not, let fire come from Abimelech and devour the men of Shechem and Beth Millo; and let fire come from the men of Shechem and from Beth Millo and devour Abimelech!* In other words, Jotham is saying to them that, "If I'm wrong in my accusations, then let there be great joy between the Shechemites and their new king Abimelech, but if my accusations are correct, let there be a mutual devastation between you."

Notice that it says that God sent a spirit of ill will upon them. God used human instrumentation in the activating of the curse sent upon the men of Shechem and Abimelech as Jotham spoke these words. This begs the question, can words do harm? The Old Testament uses at least three Hebrew verbs that can be translated as "curse" and in the English versions the word is found somewhere between 165 and 175 times or so, depending on the translation. A definition of "curse" is, "the use of powerful words to invoke supernatural harm." You may object to the idea that curses can have power over the life of a follower of the one true God but notice what it says in Proverbs 26:2, *Like a flitting sparrow, like a flying swallow, so a curse without cause shall not alight.* This verse implies that if there is any cause the curse may alight. The "cause," simply put, is a sinful pattern, either in the individual's life or in the generational flow, that has not been decisively dealt with through confession and repentance. Unconfessed sin opens the door for curses to have a negative impact in a person's life.

What was the "cause" for the men of Shechem? It was the shedding of the blood of the 70 sons of Jerubbaal. Jerubbaal is another name for Gideon, the man God used mightily. Gideon had 70 sons but another one of his sons came from his concubine and he named him Abimelek. The seventy sons were in some form of leadership and Abimelek went to the people of Shechem and asked, "Aren't you tired of having 70 men rule over you?"

The very last verse in Judges chapter nine speaks of the Curse of Jotham and the word for "curse" used here is qᵉ lälâh and this Hebrew word refers to pronouncing a formula or wishing evil on somebody, which is exactly what Jotham did. But keep in mind that just because somebody pronounces a formula, wishing evil on you doesn't mean that their words automatically have any effect. When a witch sends a curse on you it doesn't mean you're destined to suffer its consequences. If you've thoroughly dealt with the sin issues in your life and in the lives of your generations past, the curse will not impact you.

THE SIGNIFICANCY LIE

The significancy lie for the motivational gift of ruler/leader is, "I am significant when I have institutional power to build with." Consider the strain between Abimelek and his brothers. The 70 sons of Gideon were born of legitimate wives. We don't know how many wives he had but I can't imagine it being only one or two. But Abimelek, born of a concubine, was publically, explicitly, socially, and visibly not as valid or accepted as the 70 sons. He had the motivational gift of ruling and he no doubt thought that if he could obtain institutional power he could gain validation and be as good as his brothers. Another version of this lie is, "I am significant when I'm in charge of many individuals and programs." Abimelek believed the lie that he would be significant when he obtained institutional power to build with, an institution that would enable him to make changes and affect the world around him.

The bitter root underlying the Curse of Jotham is the mindset of sedition and rebellion. As seen in the story of Abimelek, sedition is the incitement or promoting of discontent or rebellion against a government in power. Another root underlying the Curse of Jotham is the attitude of entitlement. The entitlement state of mind causes people to pick leaders that they believe will give them the things they want and the residents of Shechem did exactly so. They felt they deserved it, that it was owed them. They knew that Abimelek wanted to do away with the sons of Gideon and because they wanted one man to lead them instead of 70, they selected an unscrupulous individual.

What will you experience when the Curse of Jotham is dismantled? First, you will enjoy the benefits of synergistic relationships in business, church, and other organizations you're connected to. To illustrate, you can take one horse that can pull 1,400 pounds and then another horse that can pull 1,600 pounds and put them together and you would think the maximum weight they could pull would be 3,000 pounds. But because of the principle of synergy they can pull 5,000 pounds. In other words the sum is greater than the whole of its parts. Another illustration is that you can take three cords, each strength tested to lift 100 pounds. You weave them together into a rope and combined they are able to lift 500 pounds—that's synergy. An organization affected by the Curse of Jotham witnesses an unbelievable level of ineffectiveness in the workplace. Not only is there division among the leaders, you often feel like you're walking in water up to your neck. Everything is a struggle and projects you're working on take forever to come together. The one key item you need doesn't arrive on time. You're constantly playing phone tag. The details are usually out of order and you feel as though you're wasting a lot of time. That's the fruit of the Curse of Jotham.

When you dismantle the Curse of Jotham you will begin to experience synergistic, life-giving work relationships, business relationships, or ministry relationships that enable the company or organization to reach its goals and thrive. The Curse of Jotham effectively emasculates the next generation of leadership. Not only did Abimelek die, but many of the soldiers and all of the leaders on both sides died as well. When the Curse of Jotham is in operation it seeks to destroy the next generation of leadership and that is the greatest calamity. For leaders to raise up a generation of leaders represents their greatest accomplishment.

PRAYER TO BREAK THE CURSE OF JOTHAM

"Heavenly Father, I declare that You are the God of societal structures. You are the God of institutions and You are the God of governments. I declare that You have created human institutions to be life-giving and generational. I declare that the institutions that bring death instead of life are the work of the devil and are not working according to Your original design. I ask You to open the books in my generational bloodline and identify those who operated in a spirit of ingratitude and dishonored life-giving relationships. I confess those attitudes and actions as sin and I reject and renounce them. I confess as sin the ingratitude given to those who have been life-givers. I confess, reject, and renounce the sins of sedition, lawlessness, and rebellion. I reject, renounce, break all agreements with the lie that says, "I am significant when I have power through an institution." I recognize the fact that You intended for some institutions and organizations to have enormous power and I recognize that You use organizations, businesses, and institutions to make a positive impact on social structures. But I reject the notion that significancy comes through institutional authority. Almighty God, I recognize the death that the Curse of Jotham brings but I understand that You allow this curse to take hold because of sin. It was right and just for You to empower this curse in my life and in the lives of my generations past. However, I decree and declare that through the shed blood of Jesus Christ on Calvary's cross and because of my confession, and through the power of the resurrection those iniquities are now pulled out of my body, soul, spirit, and out of my DNA. I declare that Jotham's Curse affecting my life is now halted at the cross of Christ. I ask You to cause me to walk in freedom of movement so that I can accomplish the tasks set out for me. I bless the organizations, institutions, businesses, and churches that I am assigned to. I ask for Your grace to stay faithful to the assignment You have given me even when those in authority in my life are covenant breakers. With Your help I will finish the course You have purposed me to follow. I ask You to release the blessings that have been hindered from reaching me, my ministry, my business, my family, or my institutions because of the Curse of Jotham. I ask these things in the Mighty Name of Jesus Christ, the Son of the Living God."

Chapter Sixteen
THE AMMONITE CURSE

Tᴀᴇ ꜱᴇᴠᴇɴᴛʜ ꜱɪɢɴɪꜰɪᴄᴀɴᴄʏ ᴄᴜʀꜱᴇ ɪꜱ ᴄᴀʟʟᴇᴅ ᴛʜᴇ Aᴍᴍᴏɴɪᴛᴇ Curse. Great blessings lie in store for those who break it because this curse represents the most wicked of the seven. Individuals easily fall into this one because of its subtlety and because Satan so skillfully disguises it. We find the story of its development in the book of Judges chapter 11 where we read,

> *Jephthah the Gileadite was a mighty warrior. His father was Gilead; his mother was a prostitute. ² Gilead's wife also bore him sons, and when they were grown up, they drove Jephthah away. "You are not going to get any inheritance in our family," they said, "because you are the son of another woman."³ So Jephthah fled from his brothers and settled in the land of Tob, where a gang of scoundrels gathered around him and followed him.*

> *⁴ Sometime later, when the Ammonites were fighting against Israel, ⁵ the elders of Gilead went to get Jephthah from the land of Tob. ⁶ "Come," they said, "be our commander, so we can fight the Ammonites."*

> *⁷ Jephthah said to them, "Didn't you hate me and drive me from my father's house? Why do you come to me now, when you're in trouble?"*

> *⁸ The elders of Gilead said to him, "Nevertheless, we are turning to you now; come with us to fight the Ammo-*

nites, and you will be head over all of us who live in Gilead."

⁹ Jephthah answered, "Suppose you take me back to fight the Ammonites and the LORD gives them to me—will I really be your head?"

¹⁰ The elders of Gilead replied, "The LORD is our witness; we will certainly do as you say."

¹¹ So Jephthah went with the elders of Gilead, and the people made him head and commander over them. And he repeated all his words before the LORD in Mizpah.

¹² Then Jephthah sent messengers to the Ammonite king with the question: "What do you have against me that you have attacked my country?"

¹³ The king of the Ammonites answered Jephthah's messengers,

Skip down to verse 29.

²⁹ Then the Spirit of the LORD came on Jephthah. He crossed Gilead and Manasseh, passed through Mizpah of Gilead, and from there he advanced against the Ammonites.³⁰ And Jephthah made a vow to the LORD: "If you give the Ammonites into my hands,³¹ whatever comes out of the door of my house to meet me when I return in triumph from the Ammonites will be the LORD's, and I will sacrifice it as a burnt offering."

³² Then Jephthah went over to fight the Ammonites, and the LORD gave them into his hands. ³³ He devastated twenty towns from Aroer to the vicinity of Minnith, as far as Abel Keramim. Thus Israel subdued Ammon.

³⁴ When Jephthah returned to his home in Mizpah, who should come out to meet him but his daughter, dancing to the sound of timbrels! She was an only

*child. Except for her he had neither son nor daugh-
ter. ³⁵ When he saw her, he tore his clothes and cried,
"Oh no, my daughter! You have brought me down and
I am devastated. I have made a vow to the LORD that I
cannot break."*

³⁶ *"My father," she replied, "you have given your word
to the LORD. Do to me just as you promised, now that
the LORD has avenged you of your enemies, the Ammonites. ³⁷ But grant me this one request," she said.
"Give me two months to roam the hills and weep with
my friends, because I will never marry."*

³⁸ *"You may go," he said. And he let her go for two
months. She and her friends went into the hills and wept
because she would never marry. ³⁹ After the two months,
she returned to her father, and he did to her as he had
vowed. And she was a virgin.*

*From this comes the Israelite tradition ⁴⁰ that each year
the young women of Israel go out for four days to com-
memorate the daughter of Jephthah the Gileadite.*

12 *The Ephraimite forces were called out, and they
crossed over to Zaphon. They said to Jephthah, "Why
did you go to fight the Ammonites without calling us to
go with you? We're going to burn down your house
over your head."*

² *Jephthah answered, "I and my people were engaged in
a great struggle with the Ammonites, and although I
called, you didn't save me out of their hands. ³ When I
saw that you wouldn't help, I took my life in my
hands and crossed over to fight the Ammonites, and
the LORD gave me the victory over them. Now why
have you come up today to fight me?"*

⁴Jephthah then called together the men of Gilead and fought against Ephraim. The Gileadites struck them down because the Ephraimites had said, "You Gileadites are renegades from Ephraim and Manasseh."⁵ The Gileadites captured the fords of the Jordan leading to Ephraim, and whenever a survivor of Ephraim said, "Let me cross over," the men of Gilead asked him, "Are you an Ephraimite?" If he replied, "No,"⁶ they said, "All right, say 'Shibboleth.'" If he said, "Sibboleth," because he could not pronounce the word correctly, they seized him and killed him at the fords of the Jordan. Forty-two thousand Ephraimites were killed at that time.

⁷Jephthah led Israel six years. Then Jephthah the Gileadite died and was buried in a town in Gilead (ESV).

The story of Jephthah revolves around the problem of trauma, trauma that is not self-inflicted. Sometimes I've done some pretty stupid things for which I suffered the consequences. I've sowed evil and I reaped evil. But other times I've reaped evil, suffered painfully, through no wrong doing of my own. My mother married three times, bearing children from each husband. My biological father violently beat my mother and eventually left her when I was around age two. After divorcing my father she remarried and, though he never beat her, he physically abused the children and it traumatized me to see him whipping my little brother to the point of drawing blood. That I was in an abusive environment was not my fault. I had no choice in the matter. I didn't choose my parents, nor the circumstances in which they raised me.

The problem lies, not so much in the bad things that happen to us, but in the way we respond to the bad things in our lives. I responded the wrong way toward my stepdad. I hated him to the point that if I could have killed him, and got away with it, I would have. My hatred compounded the trauma by making me an angry young man. I believed that God gave me a raw deal and I was angry with

Him and felt betrayed because in my heart I knew that God Himself had chosen my parents.

Jephthah no doubt suffered a troubling childhood as he was born of a prostitute. His father, Gilead, apparently was the most influential person in the town. He may have been named after the town or it could be that the town was named after him. To be born of a prostitute, in and of itself is not necessarily traumatic, especially if the person is raised in a rough neighborhood where other people in that locality have a comparable negative family background. But Jephthah was taken from his mother's home and reared in the home of his wealthy, influential father where his brothers and everybody in Gilead knew that he was the son of a prostitute and no doubt constantly referred to him as such. Through this stigma he had a rotten childhood.

Although the Bible does not say, his stepmother probably resented him and declined to offer him motherly nurture. We know that his brothers hated him and that he was taken away from his biological mother. We don't know if his father protected him but we do know that as an adult, after his father died, when it came time to divide the inheritance, he was cut out of the will and his brothers drove him away.

After leaving he had no place to go so he went out into the wilderness where he struggled to survive. As a rich man's son he was not mentored to enter into a trade because dad expected that Jephthah could live off his inheritance. He experienced all these difficulties through no fault or wrong doing of his own. He was dealt a bad hand. So how did he respond? He gathered around him scoundrels and went around pillaging and robbing. We could call him an outcast, a rebel, a gang leader who was the product of horrible upbringing. Where is the justice of God in this matter? Why did God allow him to be born of a prostitute and put him in a home where he received little love, in a situation he could not change? It wasn't Jephthah's choice that produced this hard life as a child.

The answer may be found in Judges 11:1, where it says "Jephthah, the Gileadite, was a mighty warrior." It is true that Jephthah was given some bad things from God that he didn't deserve, but he also received some good things from God that he didn't deserve. When he was born he did nothing at all to earn the mighty warrior gifting, but God gave that to him as well to be a part of the arrangement. Think about what the Bible means when it calls him a mighty warrior. In those day wars usually lasted only a few days. He demolished 20 towns of the Ammonites after he won the opening battle. Then the Ephraimites approached the next day with a complaint which ended in another battle. That war resulted in the loss of 42,000 Ephraimites in one day, an astounding number. To make a comparison, the US lost somewhere between 50 and 60 thousand soldiers in Vietnam over a period of 15 years. God gifted Jephthah to be a mighty warrior. He was born with the ability to lead armies much like Douglas MacArthur and George S. Patton who helped secure our freedom in WWII. And God not only created Jephthah to be a mighty warrior, He put him in the right spot at the right time so that his gifting could be utilized to free the Israelites from the Ammonites. God purposed that Jephthah be born at that time in history, to that set of parents, with that rough set of circumstances that he might be the man to lead God's people to victory.

However, there is more to the story, In Judges 11:5b we read, *"come with us to fight the Ammonites, and you will be head over all of us who live in Gilead."* Even though Jephthah was an outcast, and even though he led a group of scoundrels, even though he lived an unsanctimonious lifestyle, the elders asked him to be their commander because they recognized his gifting and, most likely, because there was no one else qualified to do the job.

Jephthah mocked the elders saying, *"Didn't you hate me and drive me from my father's house? Why do you come to me now, when you're in trouble?"* So the elders sweetened the pot by offering to make him the head over all who were in Gilead if he defeated the Ammonites. Jephthah's ears perked up at that offer and he asked for more clarity. The elders swore an oath that he would be their leader. This is where the significancy issue comes into play. God had designed Jephthah to be a military leader, not a political leader. The elders only asked him to lead the army but when he got disagreeable with them they offered him the political leadership. To his detriment, Jephthah sought to get his significancy through political leadership. Had he been a good political leader he would have assuaged the situation with the Ephraimites and avoided a civil war that cost the lives of 42,000 fellow countrymen.

It is clear that God did not call him to be a politician, He called him to be a mighty warrior. Jephthah erred when he sought after something God had not purposed for him. God planned the difficult situation in which he was raised as a child, but God was using those hard circumstances to prepare him for an amazing victory over the Ammonites. The tragedy is that he couldn't see the hand of God on his life and, out of his woundedness, his bitterness, he sought significance in the wrong place. He wanted it so badly that he made a deal with God, that if he defeated the Ammonites, he would sacrifice whatever came out of his house. As a result he lost his only child, so we see that when we seek our significance in anyone or anything other than God we usually make some very foolish decisions.

THE SIGNIFICANCY LIE

The Ammonite Curse is the seventh significancy curses and it corresponds to the seventh motivational gift, the gift of mercy. The significancy lie that the person with the gift of mercy falls into is, "I am significant when I have earned your favor." The Christianized side of this lie says, "I am significant when I have earned God's favor through extreme sacrifice." We are all created to enjoy intimacy with God but the mercy persons are able to experience intimacy more easily than the rest. However, the enemy comes along and convinces us that we must earn God's favor through our sacrifices, through our hard work.

The first indicator that a person operates under the Ammonite Curse is that their boundaries are repeatedly violated. We saw that same indicator for those under the Moabite Curse. Ammon was the younger brother of Moab and both siblings were conceived through the violation of Lot's boundaries when his daughters got him drunk in order to sleep with him. The people with the motivational gift of mercy have a tendency for their boundaries to be crossed most frequently in the area of time. They often let others disrespect their time. Because they like to please people and not offend they are at risk of being used by others.

The second indicator of the Ammonite Curse is that their quest for quality irritates those around them. It seems that an organization would be happy to have individuals who strive to produce quality work, but the Ammonite Curse is so twisted that it causes people around them to feel like their lack of diligence, their lack of excellence, is being exposed and that makes them angry. Unfortunately, the high achiever under the Ammonite Curse often gets castigated instead of praised for a job well done.

The third indicator of the Ammonite Curse is that there is a great or even excessive generosity. Individuals with the gift of mercy often give and give and give. They especially like to give to family members and to Kingdom causes. They give so extremely that it becomes inappropriate. You might ask, "What's wrong with that? Doesn't God love for us to be generous givers?" Take another look at Jephthah and see how he gave away the wherewithal that God wanted him to utilize in order to produce more resources. He gave away his daughter and in so doing he lost other resources. He lost his future son-in-law, his grandchildren, and great grandchildren. Generosity is a good and honorable trait but when we give inappropriately, without God's direction, we may be giving away the assets that God purposed for us to use in funding a mighty work He desires to do through us. We must not fall for the lie that says the more we give the more God's hand is forced to give back, as if we can control God. When Jephthah gave his daughter, a gift God did not ask for, God was not required to give him more children. Simply put, obedience is better than sacrifice.

What causes the Ammonite Curse to come into play? First, it's believing the lie that says, "I am of no value," or "I'm worthless." When you have been shamed, disgraced, or dishonored like Jephthah and you can't believe the truth about what God says about your value, you open the door for this curse to come in. When you begin to live according to other people's opinions of you, you allow the entry of the Ammonite Curse. It's necessary to clearly hear and believe what God says about you rather than the stigma others put on you.

Secondly, it's when individuals disobey man's law or God's law in order not to offend other people. Remember the story in Genesis 19 of the birth of Moab and Ben-Ammi? The oldest daughter expressed the idea of getting their father drunk so they could have intercourse with him in order to get pregnant. The older sister was the designer of this devious plan and it was she who dishonored her father's boundaries. After she followed through with the dastardly plan, the next day she encouraged her younger sister to do the same thing. The younger sister could have, and should have, said no, but she allowed the older sister to outline the scheme, and she went ahead and desecrated God's moral law concerning a father-daughter relationship. Her sin opened the door for the curse to come in. The younger sister didn't confront her older sister's sin, she was silent, she acquiesced, and passively followed the older sister's dictates in order not to offend her, to not make waves, to keep the peace. She desperately needed approval so she did what was evil to gain that approval. In a drunken stupor her father impregnated her that night and she later gave birth to a son named Ben-Ammi who became the progenitor of the Ammonite nation.

The third cause is when individuals reduce God to a procedure rather than a person. They believe that if they follow the right method, if they follow the right principles, the right steps, say the right words, give the right amount of time or money, then God is obligated to do for them what they desire. If they make a big enough sacrifice it will impress God and He will come through for them. Extreme sacrifice is not the way to enjoy an intimate relationship with the Father even though there are times when God does demand sacrifice. The original apostles and other great leaders down through history made deep sacrifices for the sake of the Kingdom and they are admired for it. But the error for many people is in believing the lie that they have to give and give and give to earn God's favor and when they fall into that trap they are acting just like Jephthah. God was going to give him the victory before he sacrificed his own daughter.

Who does God empower to break the Ammonite Curse? First, those who rise above shame, disgrace, dishonor, and trauma of childhood; those who have been stigmatized by others around them but refuse to walk in other's estimations of them. Secondly, those who seek to live such a holy life that wherever they go their presence brings conviction to others. When they walk into a room the people there stop gossiping or telling off color jokes or when others see them coming they change the TV channel to something less provocative. Thirdly, those who learn to quickly forgive themselves, who learn to be motivated by love and excitement for God, who know in their heart that they don't have to buy God's love.

REVIEW

When the Aramean Curse is eradicated you will begin to enjoy the benefit of a functional legal system. When the Moabite Curse is removed you will be able to establish proper boundaries and it will be possible to enlarge your boundaries. When the Philistine Curse is eliminated you will be enabled to enthrone Jesus on the land that He has given you, land for work or ministry. When the Canaanite Curse is broken you will be empowered to steadily grow in the areas of your greatest potential. When the Midianite Curse is eradicated you will gain the ability to accumulate resources from year to year and from generation to generation. When the Curse of Jotham is destroyed you will be empowered to construct social structures and organizations with a synergy that is life-giving. When the Ammonite Curse is eradicated you are enabled to walk in your God-ordained destiny.

PRAYER TO BREAK THE AMMONITE CURSE

"Heavenly Father, I rejoice in being able to call You Father. You are not only the Creator and the Sustainer of all things, the All-Knowing One, the Infinite One, the Holy One, the All-Sufficient One, You are my loving Father. And Father, I reject, renounce, and break all agreements with the lie that I need to earn Your favor or Your love. I reject, renounce, and break all agreements with the lie that I can reduce my relationship with You to a procedure, or a method, or a principle. I agree with You that my focus should not be on what I'm able to do for You but on You and what You want to do through me. I confess and renounce every occurrence in my generations past where one of my ancestors chose to rely on human reasoning rather than on Your wisdom. I reject, renounce, and break all agreements with the ungodly label that others have put on me. I reject, renounce, and break all agreements with the pressure others put on me to not achieve excellence. I confess as sin the coming into agreement with the fear of man and for failing to speak up against sin for fear of offending someone. I reject, renounce, and break all agreements with the sin of desiring the favor of others more than desiring to walk in the path that You, Father, have laid out for me to travel. I repent and ask for Your forgiveness. Lord, please cover these sins with Your blood in every branch of my family tree. I command every demonic spirit that gained ground by these sins to leave now and go to dry places, in Jesus' Name. I agree with You, Father, that the issue is for me to learn to love You, not for me to buy Your love through sacrifice. Anoint my eyes so that I can see Your love in a great measure throughout the day. As I see Your love please cause love to well up within me. Enlarge my heart to receive Your passion to walk in my destiny. I declare, in Jesus' Name, that the Ammonite Curse is broken in my life and in the lives of my family. I declare that the blood of Jesus has defeated this curse and that I am free, in Jesus' Name. I ask now, Father, that you would release the blessings that have been blocked due to the presence of the Ammonite Curse. Holy Spirit, I ask You to come and fill every vacated area of my life with Your Presence and Your Power. Holy Spirit, I confess that I need You, I welcome You, and I honor You. By Your grace, Heavenly Father, I will walk the path You have ordained for me, in Jesus' Name, Amen."

Part III

SPIRITUAL WARFARE OVER YOUR FINANCES

SCRIPTURE CLEARLY TEACHES THAT WE AS CHRISTIANS ARE IN A battle with the kingdom of darkness. Peter declares that our adversary, the devil, goes around seeking whom he may devour. He seeks for legal ground to bring God's people into bondage so that we can't live the life God has planned. Notice that the Bible refers to the devil as "adversary." The word "adversary" is a legal term and literally means "an opponent in a lawsuit" or "an opponent in a court of law" and he's gathering evidence against us. Once we deal with the legal ground as presented in the first sixteen chapters of this writing Satan loses his foothold and it is time to do some serious warfare over our finances.

I urge you not to pray the following warfare prayers until you have seriously addressed the sin issues. It is also imperative that you have surrendered your heart completely to the Lord Jesus Christ because only the one under authority can walk with authority. If you have already prayed a similar prayer it is okay to renew your commitment to Him by praying the following prayer.

LORDSHIP PRAYER

"Lord Jesus Christ of Nazareth, God's Son who became human flesh, I acknowledge that since You created me, and since You left heaven to be born of the virgin Mary in order to become the perfect sacrifice on Calvary's cross for my sin and the sin of humankind, and since You rose from the dead on the third day demonstrating Your authority over death itself, You have the right to be my Lord. I wholeheartedly surrender to Your Lordship. I give You all that I am. I give You my past, my present, and my future. I surrender to You all of my dreams and desires. Where You lead I will follow. I give You my heart Lord Jesus. I declare that Jesus Christ is Lord and that Jesus Christ is my Lord, Amen!"

Chapter Seventeen
JUSTICE IN
FINANCIAL MATTERS

AFTER YOU HAVE DEALT THOROUGHLY WITH THE LEGAL GROUND the enemy has gained here's what you can do when you've had finances stolen from you.

1) Go humbly before the Righteous Judge (The Most High God). We must not go before Him flippantly and with pride in our hearts. 1 Peter 5:5b-6 says, *Clothe yourselves, all of you, with humility toward one another, for "God opposes the proud but gives grace to the humble." ⁶ Humble yourselves, therefore, under the mighty hand of God so that at the proper time he may exalt you* (ESV).

    He is the Righteous Judge and His Word says, *He is the Rock, His work is perfect; for all His ways are justice, A God of truth and without injustice; righteous and upright is He* (Deut. 32:4). *He will bring justice to the poor of the people; He will save the children of the needy* (Psalm 72:4). *Righteousness and justice are the foundation of His throne* (Psalm 97:2b). Justice flows from His throne and when we meet before the Judge our defense attorney, Jesus, remains right by our side. 1 John 2:1 declares that Jesus is our advocate with the Father and the term "advocate" is another legal term and can mean "defense attorney."

2) "Most High God, based on Hebrews 10:12-22, I declare that Jesus Christ offered for all time a single sacrifice for sins, he sat

down at Your right hand, waiting for that time until His enemies should be made a footstool for His feet. I declare that by Jesus' single offering He has perfected for all time those who are being sanctified and You Father have made a covenant with me and my brothers and sisters in Christ and have put Your laws in our hearts, and wrote them on our minds. I thank You that You promised to remember our sins and lawless deeds no more."

"I thank You Father that I have confidence to enter the holy places by the blood of Jesus, by the new and living way that He opened for me through the curtain, that is, through His flesh, and since I have such a great priest over the house of God, I can draw near with a true heart in full assurance of faith, with my heart sprinkled clean from an evil conscience and my body washed with pure water."

"I thank You, Most High God, that according to Your Word in Ephesians chapters one and two, I have been chosen by You before the foundations of the world to be holy and blameless before You and that You have blessed me with every spiritual blessing in the heavenly places. I declare that as Your covenant child that it is Your purpose for me to bring praises to You. I thank You for the immeasurable greatness of Your power to me and all who believe, according to the working of Your great might that You worked in Christ when You raised Him from the dead and seated Him at Your right hand in the heavenly places, far above all rule and authority and power and dominion, and above every name that is named, not only in this age but also in the one to come. I thank You Father that You put all things under His feet and gave Him to be head over all things to the church."

"Father, I anticipate that the Accuser will argue that I was dead in my trespasses and sins and that I followed the course of this world's system, and that I carried out the passions of the flesh and because of my sin he has every right to bring me into financial bondage. I admit these accusations are true, but I thank You Father that because of Your rich mercy, and because of Your great love, even when I was dead in my trespasses and sins, You made me alive together with Christ, by Your grace I have been saved, and You raised me up with Him and seated me with Him in the heavenly places in Christ Jesus. I am Your workmanship, created in Christ Jesus for good works, which You Father prepared beforehand, that I should walk in them."

3) Accuse Satan of stealing but don't talk to Satan, talk to God. The devil did it but he used human instrumentation. Remember that Paul said we don't wrestle against flesh and blood. Say, "Righteous Judge, I come before You humbly as your blood-bought, covenant child, beseeching You for justice. Satan has stolen from me in _____."
(Describe the way in which he stole from you.)

4) Ask Him for divine retribution and justice. Say, "Lord, I don't come demanding but humbly asking You, as my loving Heavenly Father and Righteous Judge of heaven and earth, for retribution and justice on my behalf."

5) The retribution asked for is that amount times seven as found in Proverbs 6:30-31 where we read, *People do not despise a thief if he steals to satisfy himself when he is starving. Yet when he is found, he must restore sevenfold; he may have to give up all the substance of his house.* Say this, "Lord the devil came to steal, kill, and destroy and he has stolen from me. He has stolen from me through (Tell God again how he stole from you _____.)
Righteous Judge of the heaven and earth, I ask You to make him repay me sevenfold, in Jesus' Name."

6) Bind all the demons from further operation in this matter. Say, "In the Name of Jesus, I bind all demons who are involved in this injustice from further operation in this matter."

7) Receive the judgment you asked for. Say, "Lord, I receive the judgment requested, in Jesus' Name."

8) Bless the human instruments known and unknown that were involved in this loss. Say, "I bless the human instruments known

and unknown that were involved in this loss. I bless
_____." (Name all those that you know who
were involved.) "I bless them with seeing eyes, hearing ears, and
a heart to know and understand the truth of God."

9) Thank God for your recovery. You don't need to do the above
eight steps repeatedly but continue to thank God every day for
His justice.

10) You may want to write these out and sign the document and
date it, thus, making it a "memorial stone" to help you remember what you asked for and when.

This _____ *(day) of* _____ *(month)*
_____ *(year) I* _____ *(full
name) solemnly and with great reverence came before the Righteous Judge of heaven and earth, with Jesus Christ as my defense
attorney, and accused Satan of stealing my financial blessings.
Since I have confessed my sins and the sins of my ancestors, and
since I have forgiven the human instruments involved, and since
I have broken all inner vows, lies, and expectancies related to finances, and since Jesus' blood is sufficient in washing away all sin
and iniquity, Satan no longer has legal ground to devour my finances. I declare that the thief has to repay me sevenfold as I receive the judgment requested, in Jesus' Name.*

_____ *(signature)*

Chapter Eighteen
A WARFARE STRATEGY

1) Read aloud Isaiah 41:10-13, *Fear not, for I am with you; be not dismayed, for I am your God. I will strengthen you, yes, I will help you, I will uphold you with My righteous right hand.*[11] *Behold, all those who were incensed against you shall be ashamed and disgraced; they shall be as nothing, and those who strive with you shall perish.* [12] *You shall seek them and not find them—those who contended with you. Those who war against you shall be as nothing, as a nonexistent thing.* [13] *For I, the LORD your God, will hold your right hand, saying to you, "Fear not, I will help you."*

2) Say this with authority: "I stand on these verses. I enforce this on you demons who are making this happen. (Don't address Satan but only low-level demons). I say your operation against me is destroyed and dissolved. And you who have striven with me become as nothing now!!! Become as a nonexistent thing!!!"

3) Do steps 1 and 2 every day until you see a breakthrough.

DECLARATIONS OVER FINANCES

Using the Bible as a sword by speaking regular positive declarations over your finances can have a powerful impact on your life and your financial situation. Scripture says that death and life are in the power of the tongue and in this context I underscore the word "life." Not only do negative words bring death, positive words bring life and when God said that He meant it. This exercise is not a "name it and claim it" scheme to get rich. It is a simple matter of declaring

God's Word and there's power in the Word. Here are some Biblical declarations to proclaim daily. Attach each of the following declarations to a separate index card. Make the declarations out loud and hold the card up to the Lord and praise God until you get a peace or release in your spirit. Do this every day and guard your mouth so that you don't speak curses on your finances through critical words and grumbling and complaining. Keep in mind that you are not trying to manipulate God; you are standing on His promises and doing warfare against the enemy.

"I honor the Lord with my substance and with the first fruits of my increase. My barns are filled with plenty, and my presses burst forth with new wine" (Proverbs 3:9-10).

"My God makes all grace abound toward me in every favor and earthly blessing, so that I have all sufficiency for all things and abound to every good work" (2 Cor. 8:9).

"In Jesus' Name, I declare that I have extraordinary uncommon wisdom in managing and investing my finances. I am filled with the wisdom of God, and I am led to make wise and prosperous financial decisions" (Proverbs 4:6-8).

"The Spirit of God guides me into all truth regarding my financial affairs" (John 16:13).

"There is no lack, for my God supplies all my needs according to His riches in glory by Christ Jesus" (Phil. 4:19).

"The Lord has pleasure in the prosperity of His servant, and Abraham's blessings are mine" (Psalm 35:27; Gal. 3:14).

Part *IV*

PRACTICAL MATTERS

Chapter Nineteen
Ten Tips To Saving Money

1) **Learn to live by a budget.**

Write down your monthly expenses, category-by-category and add up your spending totals. Write down your monthly income totals. For those who earn an income through commissions the monthly amount will vary so you have to do some averaging. Guess what? You're on your way to building a budget. Budget templates can be found online for free or you can purchase budget software. Whatever you do develop a budget and stick to it. Dave Ramsey offers free downloadable budget forms and an online budgeting portal. Dave's online budgeting service presents a free level and an upgraded paid level.

For new homebuyers it's tempting to spend a ton of money right away because you're excited about all the decorating you want to do. Instead of buying everything all at once, it would be better to pace yourself by only buying a few items that you absolutely need to have right away. You may need an accountability partner who will hold you accountable for all your purchases especially if you have a history of reckless spending.

2) **Learn to coupon.**

When Ruthie and I go out to eat with another couple I'm amazed at those who are diligent to bring a coupon, and their bill ends up being a lot lower than mine. Frankly, I usually don't spend the time and effort to find the right coupons but I need to do it regularly if I want to save a significant amount of money over the course of a year. We should try to shop at places where coupons are welcomed. Before going to a store, search the weekly ad circulars for special deals making sure you're getting the best price.

3) Rethink the way you spend money.

Get this aphorism in your heart, "If you don't need it, don't buy it." This will help you to rethink the way you spend money. Take a serious look at your monthly spending, carefully going over every expenditure and determine where you can cut back. Every buck you don't use up now is another buck you can use later for more important items.

4) Learn to be energy efficient.

Small changes can reap big rewards. Strive to save water by cutting down the time each family member showers. You can even buy water saving shower heads. This may seem like an inconvenience but over a year's time you will save a lot of money on your water bills to say nothing of the money saved on heating the water. While brushing your teeth, run the water while rinsing but turn it off while brushing.

Turn the lights off when you leave the room. Install a motion sensor for the light on your front porch so that if you forget to turn the light switch off the light will go off automatically. When selecting an electric company keep in mind the difference between a bundled rate and an unbundled rate. The salesman may tell you, for example, that your rate will be eight cents per kilowatt hour. But he fails to inform you that his quote does not include the energy provider company's fees so that in essence you're really paying 12 cents per kilowatt hour. His rate is an unbundled rate.

Put extra insulation in the attic. Sometimes there are government programs that install insulation for free or for little cost.

5) Eat at home.

With our busy schedules these days life can get hectic. You may be working full time, going to college part time, and running a household and it's easy to just say, "Let's go out to eat." I know people that spend between $500 and $1,000 a month on eating out because it's convenient. But you can fix your own meals if you're willing to make some adjustments such as planning, preparing, and cooking the meals for the entire week. You can cook good healthy meals that energize your body and soul.

Even forgoing eating out at the pricey places and dropping by the cheap to-go restaurant those bills can add up. When I think about how often my wife and I eat at one of our favorite quick, to-go spots, we could easily save almost $20 - $50 a week. That adds up to around $86 - $217 a month and $1,040 to $2,600 a year!

When you do eat out drink water instead of other beverages. Water is not only good for your health it's easy on the pocketbook. Restaurants jack up the price of soft drinks astronomically over what it costs them. You and your spouse can easily save five dollars on a meal if you only drink water.

Share meals. One 20 oz. steak divided two ways costs less than two separate 10 oz. steak dinners. The waiter will be happy to bring an extra plate so you can cut the steak in half and share. In addition to saving money this practice also helps with the waste line.

If you must eat out before leaving your home check online for any coupons for the restaurant you're going to.

6) Do your own yard work if you are physically able.

Homeowners want their yard to look as nice as their neighbors. When it comes to lawn care you may think that you're too busy so you hire a professional who will keep up your yard on a regular basis. Why not forgo the gym workout once a week and mow the lawn instead. It's good exercise and could save you $130 to $200 per month depending on the size of your property. You may think about enlisting the help of a teenager or someone in the neighborhood if time is an issue. In this way you can save thousands of dollars a year.

7) Do some of the home projects yourself.

One thing I've experienced as a homeowner is there's always a project —whether it's modernizing your kitchen, painting the walls, remodeling your bathroom, or installing new flooring. To keep costs down do what you can do. For example, most people can paint. Doing your own painting can save thousands of dollars.

8) Stay out of debt.

In 2015 the average American household spent $6,658 in interest. That's in one year! Think of what you could do with an extra six or seven thousand dollars. Here is a simple principle: when you spend more than you make you acquire debt. Pray for discipline to hold off on purchases until you have saved the money to pay in cash. Bill Hybels says that discipline is delayed gratification. Delayed gratification in money matters is the ability to resist the temptation to spend money on an immediate reward and wait for a bigger reward later. That means you need to make a plan to save up enough money so you can pay in cash.

Make a list of the items you want to buy. Separate these short-term goals into "necessity" and "wish" lists. If your furnace is about to go kerflooey fixing or replacing that would be a necessity. That new thingamabob you want for your workshop or game room probably should go on the wish list. Then write down your long-term goals and list them in the order of importance, things such as a college fund for your kids, and retirement. Lay out plans to actually reach the most important goals. Estimating tools can be found online to help you calculate how much you will need to retire.

In my opinion buying a home is a justifiable reason for incurring debt. The reason I say this is for two reasons. First, you have to have a place to live. Spending money on a mortgage makes more sense for most people than spending money on rent. Of course it depends on your circumstances but what I'm saying is that I don't believe it's necessarily wrong to go into debt to buy a home. It's only wrong if you buy a house you can't afford. Second, the home becomes a major investment and homes histori-cally appreciate in value. Another justifiable reason for incurring debt is for health reasons. Hospitals can charge mega-bucks for needed surgical procedures and even if you have health insurance, insurance companies don't always pay 100% which leaves you with a sizable debt. But what can you do especially if it's a matter of life or death?

9) Buy a used car rather than a new one.

On average, a new car will lose as much as 19 percent of its value in its first year of ownership. That means that your $30,000 new car will be worth about $24,300 after just one year. The value of your new car decreases significantly with each successive year. The newer the car the faster the rate of depreciation. On average a new car loses 11% of its value the moment you drive it off the car lot. Think of it! Your $30,000 car loses $3,300 just by virtue of driving it off the lot! I'm not suggesting that you have to buy an old clunker but what I am saying is that you will save a lot of money by purchasing a very nice car with low mileage that's just a year or two old.

10) Build an emergency cash fund.

I suggest that you save up an amount equal to three to six months of average living expenses in case you are out of work for one reason or another or a major problem arises in your home. This money should be placed in an account that allows you ac-cess to these funds in case of an emergency with no penalty. For emergencies, accessibility is paramount. For example, if your heating and air conditioner unit goes kerflooey you don't want to wait a week or two to get the money to pay for a new one. You never know when the vicissitudes of life will throw you a curve ball and when this happens don't get stuck with having to go into debt. It may take you a while to build the emergency cash fund but you can do it with God's help if you are persistent.

My mother-in-law lost her husband through a tragic accident while she was in her twenties. She was left to support her family of four children by working on a chicken ranch in Southern California. I don't think she made a ton of money but she lived by a simple principle, give God the first ten percent, save ten percent, and live off the rest. This plan worked well for her all of her life and even though she never became a "wealthy" person, she and her family always had enough and she never went into debt.

TRAINING IN MONEY MANAGEMENT

I highly recommend that you take Dave Ramsey's Financial Peace University course. He will teach you life-changing practical matters in managing your finances. Dave Ramsey teaches that we start debt reduction by taking the smallest debt and paying all of the extra money toward it until it is paid off. By focusing all of our efforts on the smallest debt produces the best results and he calls this the "snowball method." After we pay that bill off then concentrate on the next smallest debt, and so on. Ramsey's method helps us not to see an overwhelming mountain of debt, but one debt at a time. You may need to make use of a financial life coach. These coaches may be found through Dave Ramsey's organization.

I also recommend a course that my church uses fairly regularly entitled "Managing Our Finances God's Way" by Rick Warren.

I urge you to read Robert Morris' book, *The Blessed Life*. Many people have testified of the tremendous impact this book has had upon their life.

Also, Jeff Yeager's book, *How to Retire the Cheapskate Way* offers good advice for retirees cutting down their expenses.

END NOTES

1 *Theological Wordbook of the Old Testament*, The Moody Bible Institute of Chicago, copyright©1980

2 Prayer adapted from Vision Life Ministries Freedom and Fullness Seminar syllabus

3 Paul Cox, *Generational Deliverance, 2015 Edition,* Copyright©2015, www.aslansplace.com

4 John deGraaf, David Wann, Thomas H. Naylor, Berrett-Koehier Publishers, Inc. Copyright©2014

5 Arthur Burk tells the story that he and his wife faithfully tithed and gave offerings above the tithe for many years. Despite his obedience in giving his family struggled financially. For him it was a seasonal devouring. They were careful about how they spent money and were able to manage to get ahead but then at a certain time of the year the devouring came and their money vanished and they went back to square one. This scenario continued to play out year after year. Then someone suggested that he see a Sally Beckmon for personal ministry. When he explained his situation with her she said, "It sounds like you have the Midianite Curse." Arthur had never heard of the Midianite Curse prior to that moment but he allowed her to minister to him in that area. After ministry Arthur knew that a definite shift took place and since that time the seasonal devourings have ceased.

This experience proved to be a defining moment for Arthur. He thought that if the Midianite Curse had such a powerful negative effect on his finances, then maybe there are more curses found in the book of Judges that needed his attention. For him the Lord began to illuminate the subject until Arthur discovered the seven curses and how they relate to the seven motivational or redemptive gifts and also to the other "sevens" found throughout Scripture.

I asked Arthur Burk if I could include his material in this book. He gave me permission only if I put it in my own words. To honor Arthur I have eliminated some of the "Arthurisms" and most of his personal stories. I use my own terminology in most cases, for example, Arthur uses the term "legitimacy curses" and "legitimacy lies." Instead, I use the term "significancy curses" and "significancy lies." He calls the seven gifts listed in Romans chapter twelve "Redemptive Gifts." I call them "Motivational gifts" because that was the term I learned over 30 years ago when I first began to study the spiritual gifts. I like the term "Motivational" because I've seen that these gifts become the primary motivation behind the way we approach life and ministry.

My version is much shorter than Arthur's because it does not contain most of his personal stories. This is a good thing because, although my version, I believe, contains the necessary truths to break these curses, my version takes much less time to go through the material. I have been ministering to people the teachings and exercises in this book on a one-on-one basis for quite some time but my desire was to develop a one-day workshop to cover all or most of the material.

My wife and I discovered Arthur's teaching around eight years ago from the time of this writing. We prayed the prayers of confession and renunciation and their effects were so subtle that we didn't see the connection at first. As time went along, however, it became clear that there was a definite shift in our lives financially beginning about the time we prayed Arthur's prayers.

Since then I have come to see that there are a whole lot of other factors involved in bringing healing to our financial life. Curses take effect in our lives through sin, either our sins or the sins of our ancestors. These sins must be confessed and renounced because the curses don't automatically get broken once we are saved. So the first half of this book focuses primarily on seeking wisdom, confessing and breaking agreements with sin, breaking word curses, breaking inner vows, lies, and expectancies, and learning true contentment.

[6] Arthur Burk refers to these curses as "legitimacy curses."

[7] Arthur Burk and others refers to the seven gifts listed in Romans 12 as "Redemptive Gifts."

CPSIA information can be obtained
at www.ICGtesting.com
Printed in the USA
BVHW041544080319
542132BV00002B/116/P

9 780979 060748